Our insatiable lust for anything and e[illegible] Redeemer is treason! Bigney captures the essence of this gospel reality through biblical exposition and personal stories. *Gospel Treason* rightly confronts our ongoing heart struggles and offers hope through the gospel of Jesus Christ. You will be blessed by reading, reflecting, and applying the truths found in this book written from the heart of a pastor.

—**Robert Cheong**, Pastor of Care and Counseling, Sojourn Community Church

Brad has thought a lot about the insidiousness of idolatry in today's culture. He has done a thorough job of showing us how modern-day idols are both offensive to God and grace-robbing to the believer. This book will cause you to consider your own heart in terms of what you really want and live for. It will also help you to minister to others who are suffering or caught in sin that hinders them from the freedom we have in the gospel.

—**Garrett Higbee**, Director, Biblical Soul Care, Harvest Bible Chapel

From a rich background of personal struggle and pastoral ministry, Pastor Brad Bigney will help you understand what motivates your desires, thinking, emotions, and behavior. As you read, you will begin to understand your own struggle, the power of the gospel to help you grow and change, and what (or Who) should be your true treasure: Jesus Christ.

—**Kevin Carson**, Biblical Counseling Professor, Baptist Bible College and Graduate School

In *Gospel Treason* Brad unmasks my idolatrous heart and reveals God's glorious gospel. He tears down what has been hindering me and gives me what I really need. This book makes me want to haul the idols of my heart to the nearest landfill and it makes me want to live for God's glory and honor, rejoicing in his wonderful love. Read it and let it do the same for you.

—**Amy Baker**, Counselor, Faith Biblical Counseling Ministries

Brad Bigney writes with insight, transparency, and candor on a topic that each of us needs to carefully think about. Bigney gleans great truth from the top theologians of the day and organizes it in a way that is easy to understand, clear, and applicable. This book would be a great help to anyone who wants to more deeply understand how to walk in integrity with God.

—**Jocelyn Wallace**, Executive Director, Vision of Hope Residential Treatment Center

It is always good when God arranges for my eyes to read the words that my heart needs to hear! *Gospel Treason* does just this. Brad Bigney has reminded us that the problems we all face are rarely superficial and that we must get to the heart issues. This book clearly tells us how to identify and deal with the things we choose to worship instead of God.

—**Charles D. Hodges Jr.**, Director of Grace Counseling, Grace Church

Brad is very transparent and writes in a way that is easy to understand and easy to apply.

—**Stuart Scott**, Executive Director, National Center of Biblical Counseling

Brad's outstanding examples, illustrations and stories make the concepts he is teaching clear and concrete, while also making the book fun to read.

—**Jim Newheiser**, Director, Institute for Biblical Counseling and Discipleship

I will give the book to friends and use it as assigned reading in my counseling.

—**Randy Patten**, Executive Director, National Association of Nouthetic Counselors

Let these important words guide you as you continue to mature in your relationship with Jesus.

—**Stephen Viars**, Senior Pastor, Faith Church

GOSPEL TREASON

Betraying the Gospel with Hidden Idols

BRAD BIGNEY

Italics within Scripture quotations indicate emphasis added.

ISBN: 978-1-59638-402-6 (pbk)
ISBN: 978-1-59638-550-4 (ePub)
ISBN: 978-1-59638-549-8 (Mobi)

Printed in the United States of America

To my precious wife,
Vicki,
and our five children
for being both the channels and the crucible
in which God keeps teaching me these life-changing truths.

My life is so much richer because of each of you.

CONTENTS

If you have any questions or comments regarding this book, I'd love to hear from you. You can contact me at bradbigney@graceky.org or Twitter@ BradBigney.

ADDITIONAL RESOURCES FOR *GOSPEL TREASON*

- Free study guide with discussion questions for each chapter
- Free *Gospel Treason* video sermons
- Free *Gospel Treason* audio sermons

Go to www.bradbigney.com to download a free guide for leading a small group or Sunday school class on this book, as well as free video and audio sermons that complement the book's theme.

ACKNOWLEDGMENTS

Special thanks to my assistant, Laura Lewis, for the hours she spent in formatting and sharpening the final manuscript. Also, without the enthusiasm of my former assistant, Marina Smirenski, who invested hours and hours in preparing proposals and sending them to publishers, this book would still be just a computer file. Meghan Krusling did the initial hard work in the trenches of cleaning up the original sermon transcriptions to bring them more in line with the written English language. And after I'd given up hope and set the project aside, God raised up Robert and Billie Gentry for a labor of love, as they invested hours to take what I'd written and make it so much better! Without their special touch, publishers would still be saying, "Thanks, but no thanks." But most of all, without the persistence of my beautiful helpmeet, Vicki, these messages would never have moved from my life to my lips in a sermon series. Thank you for asking me year after year, "When are you going to preach on idols of the heart?" And then for giving me the loving shove to set aside time to actually put it into book form. Once again, God used you to lead me into something life-changing. You're the best!

Little of the content in this book is my own. It's flowed through me but didn't start with me. I'm indebted to so many others who for the past twenty years have taught me so much about the gospel and issues of the heart. So I wrote this book while standing on the shoulders of David Powlison, Paul Tripp, Ed Welch, and so many other biblical counselors who have gone before me and tilled the ground on this issue of the heart. Thank you for changing my life and ministry by helping me to better understand why I do what I do. I also owe a debt of gratitude to C. J. Mahaney for his life-changing sermon series *The Idol Factory*, and for living a life that is worthy of following. He's mentored me for years through his books and sermons without ever having met me. But most of all I thank God for using my dear friend Stuart Scott to do more than write about idols of the heart. He became my "Nathan" and sat across from Vicki and me twenty years ago, opening God's Word to counsel us on our marriage and showing us for the very first time so many of the concepts I'm sharing in this book. God used you, Stuart, to do more than just save a marriage; you redefined and redirected the course of my ministry to the glory of God!

Huge thanks goes to Marvin Padgett and the team at P&R Publishing for being excited about this project and for taking a chance on a new author. It's been a joy to partner with you on this book.

Finally, I thank God for the way he's used my Grace Fellowship church family to teach me the truths in this book. What a joy it has been to change and grow with you, as well as love and lead you, for these sixteen years. A special thanks to each one who allowed his or her personal testimony to be shared in these chapters.

Coram Deo.

INTRODUCTION

My wife and I have been married for twenty-five years, but twenty years ago we were at war. There was no camouflage, there were no guns, and neither of us was crawling under barbed wire in our single-wide mobile home. But we both felt that we were constantly stepping on land mines in our relationship—putting out brushfires, running for cover, and dodging the bullets that our tongues fired back and forth. Our marriage had deteriorated into a battlefield, and we were opposing forces.

And the casualty rate was high.

The love and laughter that had initially filled our home, and had characterized our courtship, seemed like a distant memory, and I began to wonder whether those early years had even been real. Maybe we had been fooling ourselves back then; maybe there was no such thing as real love. Maybe what we had was as good as it got. And yet I sensed that God wanted more for us, both for our good and for his glory.

My wife and I seemed worlds apart, but neither of us could say what had gone wrong. What had been our first misstep? Where had we wandered off the path of marital bliss? And how had this relationship—one that God had designed to be our greatest earthly comfort—turned into all-out war?

For countless hours we argued in circles, each defending ourselves and blaming the other. We solicited help from older couples, hoping they could help us to sort out where our marriage had gone wrong.

In every case, they were gracious and offered us a thread of biblical truth, such as: "You both just need to die to self." But no one could penetrate the surface of our skirmishes; no one could unearth our hearts' foundations and expose the real problem—*idolatry*.

We had abandoned the gospel as our first love, and had instead begun to treasure and cling to something else as our reason for living. We were traitors—turncoats—who had given something other than Jesus Christ and his sweet gospel first place in our hearts, and the result was havoc in our home.

The ripples of our idolatry crashed into each other, as from two large rocks dropped into opposite ends of a quiet pond. But neither of us knew how to calm the waters again.

By God's mercy we eventually found a biblical counselor, and things began to change radically. Not that he introduced us to the gospel—we had both been Christians from a young age. I was the pastor of a local church; we still read our Bibles and prayed; neither of us had knowingly abandoned the faith—but we had replaced our Savior with idols, and these became the driving force in our hearts. We had fallen into the trap that God warned his people about so many years ago when he said, "For My people have committed two evils: They have forsaken Me, the fountain of living waters, and hewn themselves cisterns—broken cisterns that can hold no water" (Jer. 2:13).

We had spent a lifetime digging other cisterns, from which we hoped to catch life-giving water to sustain us, fulfill us, and bring us peace and joy. And the digging didn't start on our wedding day—it had been going on for years. We simply imported the project into our marriage. The pressures of marriage and ministry, along with the close proximity of another sinner, simply pushed to the surface what had been lurking in our hearts all along.

So if you and your spouse or you and someone else are where we were almost twenty years ago, you might be saying, "Help us!

What did the counselor say that made such a difference? What did you learn from God's Word that so transformed your marriage?"

That is exactly what I want to share with you in the chapters that follow.

The breakthrough for us came when the counselor helped us to identify—and repent of—the ways in which we had allowed other desires, other goals, and other cravings to dethrone our Savior and his gospel—the ways in which we had allowed these idols to become entrenched and to rule in his place.

He taught us from Ezekiel 14 and James 4:1–3 about the idols of our hearts—this was news to both of us. Neither of us had gone to a counselor believing ourselves to be idolaters—we just knew we had a bad marriage, and we each believed the other was the one who needed to change. We had both grown up in church, but had never been taught the dangers of having something other than Jesus Christ and his gospel rule our hearts.

My "Aha!" moment came when the truth came crashing down on me that what I was chasing after in my heart ("I must be well thought of by everyone at church") had a direct impact on not only the way I treated my wife, but also my daily, moment-by-moment decisions. And exposing the idols of my heart helped me to take giant steps toward resolving the ongoing conflicts in our marriage. It shifted the target of my attack away from my wife and onto my heart, so that I could begin to work on more than just trying to "be nice," or to be polite, or to have a date night.

Brought face-to-face with the ugly monster that was my own idolatrous heart, I found freedom in seeing the real enemy for the first time. It humbled me, and it heightened my love and appreciation for the gospel and my Savior. It has deepened my awareness of my dependence on Christ to rule my life moment by moment.

And it's been hard.

The valley indeed was dark, but God has done an incredible work, not only in our marriage (we are now the best of friends, as well as lovers!), but also in the way I preach and teach, and how I relate to others, both inside and outside our church family. I am reminded of Ephesians 3:20, seeing that God really is "able to do exceedingly abundantly above all that we ask or think." My wife and I had desperately wanted deliverance from a marriage that we felt trapped in, but God did more—he revolutionized our ministry and our passion for the gospel, for our Savior, and for the church.

I pray that God will use this book to help get the life-changing message of exposing and repenting of idols of the heart into the hands of as many people as possible.

In the chapters ahead, I will lay out a plan to help you identify and destroy the idols that keep you enslaved to certain sins in your life, sins that keep you from experiencing gospel joy and freedom. I will show you how to keep the main thing the main thing. But I warn you, it's not fun. It will hurt, and it will get ugly when you start to see what is going on in your heart.

Look to Christ. Don't let this study turn you into a navel-gazer who is more caught up in examining your own heart than in delighting in your Savior. Fix your eyes on Christ, and on the wonders that he has secured for you, as you step into the dark labyrinth of your heart.

So before we begin, stop and pray that God will show you more of the beauty of your Savior, even as he reveals more of the ugliness and deception of your idolatrous heart.

If you have any questions or comments regarding the book, I'd love to hear from you. You can contact me at bradbigney@graceky.org or Twitter@BradBigney. You can also go to my website at www.bradbigney.com to download a free study guide for the book, as well as listen to free audio sermons that complement its theme.

PART 1

SO WHAT'S THE PROBLEM?

CHAPTER 1

IDOLATRY STARTS WITH GOSPEL DRIFT

A biblical understanding of idolatry dramatically changed my own life and exposed how far I had drifted from the gospel. It radically changed my understanding of everything—my marriage, my parenting, my pastoring, and my counseling. Idolatry is perhaps the Bible's most pervasive theme. We think of the great themes in Scripture: the grace of God, the glory of God, the sovereignty of God. We love to talk about these (as we should), but there's another, largely untapped, theme whose threads are woven throughout the Bible: idols of the heart. And this idolatry flies in the face of our Savior and the freedom that he purchased for us on the cross.

To move toward idols is to move away from the gospel and the Savior that the gospel proclaims, so the problem is not peripheral—it is central. Anything that prevents the gospel from having center stage in your life will dramatically affect the way you live and hinder the degree to which you can glorify God. And when the gospel loses center stage, your spiritual immune system shuts down, leaving you susceptible to a myriad of spiritual illnesses.

That's why, in 1 Corinthians 15:1–3, Paul stresses the priority of the gospel:

> Now, brothers, I want to remind you of the gospel I preached to you, which you received and on which you have taken your stand. . . .
>
> For what I received I passed on to you as of first importance: that Christ died for our sins according to the Scriptures. (NIV)

C. J. Mahaney said, "If there's anything in life that we should be passionate about, it's the gospel. . . . I mean passionate about thinking about it, dwelling on it, rejoicing in it, allowing it to color the way we look at the world. Only one thing can be of first importance to each of us. And only the gospel ought to be."[1]

IDOLS MOVE IN WHEN THE GOSPEL MOVES OUT

Yet countless Christians live every day with something other than the gospel holding first place in their lives. When I say *idolatry*, you might think, "That's the Old Testament. As the New Testament church, we're under grace." Is that what comes to your mind? Do you think of idolatry as existing only in the Old Testament? Or do you think of some statue or totem pole, and someone in a third-world country bowing down to it? Do you ever think of yourself? If not, therein lies the problem.

Biblical counselor and author David Powlison observes, "Idolatry is by far the most frequently discussed problem in the Scriptures. The relevance of massive chunks of Scripture hangs on our understanding of idolatry."[2]

IDOLATRY IS A PERVASIVE PROBLEM TODAY

But if you're still thinking, "Sure, idolatry's a big deal, but it's in the Old Testament, not where I live," then look at just one verse in the little New Testament book of 1 John, the very last verse. It is worth noting how John ends his letter. After giving us 105 verses on the vital importance of a warm, vibrant, loving fellowship with Christ our Savior, how does the apostle of love wrap it all up? Of all the ways he could have ended this passionate letter, he closes it, in 1 John 5:21, with this sober warning: "Little children, keep yourselves from idols. Amen."

So what have you been doing with this verse? Have you been skipping over it, ignoring it, or wondering why it's there? Did John lose his train of thought? Is he changing subjects? Is it a scribal error? Not at all. You see, gospel treason—gospel drift—inevitably leads to idolatry. We are worshipers by nature. Our hearts don't just drift aimlessly; the drift is always away from the gospel, away from our Savior, and into the grip of something or someone else.

The last little line in John's letter leaves us asking the most basic question of all, the question that God brings to our hearts every moment of every day: Has something or someone besides Jesus Christ taken the title deed to your heart? Does something or someone else hold your heart's trust, loyalty, and desire?

You say, "Of course not. I put my trust in Christ when I became a Christian. He holds the deed to my heart." Unfortunately, many times, although Christ owns the property, we live like traitors, having given the right of ownership to other people and other things. Yes, Christ is the owner, and that will be evident when the dust settles. But we are prone to giving our hearts to squatters all the time. That's why John leaves us with this warning: *Keep yourselves from idols.*

Don't give your heart away like a spiritual orphan or prostitute.

The Christian life is more than just trying to stay connected to Christ and loving him. If you don't also keep a vigilant eye toward detecting idols and then destroying them, you'll inevitably get trapped.

You might confess with your lips, "Jesus is Lord," but in your functional, practical life, what really motivates you? Most of us have a confessional theology that looks good and lines up with sound biblical doctrine, but what really drives us on Monday morning is our practical or functional theology—which can be way out of line. You might say, "Jesus is Lord," but in your life—your thoughts and your desires and your affections—you might be dominated by something such as winning your husband's approval, moving up the company ladder, or having the perfect family. If so, you're only fooling yourself, because these other things are really your lord, your idol—the gospel and Jesus Christ have been pushed to the margins. That other person, idea, or dream is your master, and it takes you over without your being aware of it.

OUR IDOLATRY FLIES UNDER THE RADAR

Nobody wakes up one day and says, "I'm going to start living for the approval and affection of my husband. That will be my ruling passion starting right now, and I will refuse to find comfort in God, his Word, and his promises until I get the approval and affection from my husband that I crave." Nobody voices that thought out loud. Nobody types that up and makes copies to hand out to friends and family and coworkers. Even so, you have made a definite switch that affects how you think and act toward others. And that's why your behavior and attitudes are so confusing to those around you.

Millions of people—including Christians—live this way without even knowing it. They're trapped, they're deceived, and they're miserable because they have made a functional god of something or someone other than the one true living God, which leads to misery and chaos every time. Part of what makes this battle so tough is that we don't recognize the idolatry we've bought in to. We recognize the misery and the chaos, so we ramp up the prayers—and usually the complaining—but after a while, when we are still miserable, we start to doubt God's faithfulness and the power of prayer because he's not helping us to get what we want.

But unlike us, God sees perfectly. We don't see that what we're asking God to give us is an idol, but he does. He sees that we've shifted from the gospel and our Savior as our sole source of joy and purpose. God won't help us to chase our idols. He is a jealous God. In Isaiah 42:8, he proclaims, "I *am* the LORD, that is My name; and My glory I will not give to another, nor My praise to carved images." When God sees you pursuing the glory of another, he's not going to help you get it. Pray all you want, fast, give up your favorite desserts and snack foods, all to no avail—because God smells idolatry.

So why don't we smell it?

God has given us his Word to serve as smelling salts, to rouse us from the idolatrous coma we live in so much of the time. We're locked into our own idolatrous way of thinking and living until we pick up God's Word, and then, *boom!* A wake-up call—we've been seeing things wrong; we haven't had the complete picture. There's truth in the Scripture that hasn't been on the table of our mind. And God's Word brings us back to the Savior, back to the gospel.

If you haven't figured it out yet, Christ is the main character of the Bible, and redemption—the gospel—is the theme. Why? Because God knows that we drift and need to be brought back again and again to the Savior, and to the sin-shattering, idol-smashing gospel.

IDOLATRY IS A LIFELONG BATTLE

Now, before you get too excited about coming back to your Savior, getting back to the gospel, and dealing with idols of your heart—and I hope you are excited about it—let me give you a caution. Don't think, "Great—this is the day I slay all the idols of my heart. As soon as I figure out what they are, I'll have an incredible revival service and repent of them all and be done with it. I'll park myself at the feet of Jesus, like Mary in Luke 10, and never leave. No need to read the rest of *this* book, because that will be it; I'll be done."

I wish that were true. But you must understand that detecting and destroying idols is an ongoing battle, not a showdown. You'll have plenty of showdowns, to be sure. But it will be tough, because idols don't go to the mat easily. They don't just give up. It's better to think in terms of a war with multiple showdowns for as long as Christ leaves you in this life.

Jeremiah 17:9 says, "The heart is . . . desperately wicked; who can know it?" That's why this battle can't be won with some cute little Christian techniques or tricks that you can pick up at your local Christian bookstore. It can be won only with the sword of the Spirit, as the Word of God cuts through our heart's protective layers to expose and excise what's really going on, so that real change can begin. You must focus on God's Word rather than techniques or principles. Make God's Word your focus for freedom from idols.

James 4:1–3 gives the plain truth:

> Where do wars and fights come from among you? Do they not come from your desires for pleasure that war in your members? You lust and do not have. You murder and covet and cannot obtain. You fight and war. Yet you do not have because you do not ask. You ask and do not receive, because you ask amiss, that you may spend it on your pleasures.

Notice in this passage how prayer is tied in to the deal. So many times when we're not getting an answer to prayer, we get frustrated and think, "Hey, I'm not asking God to give me a casino or a porn shop, so he should give me what I want. What I want is good. I want godly kids. I want my husband to treat me as Ephesians 5 says he's supposed to." Well, guess what? We ask amiss, because so often we want something just because it would make our lives more comfortable.

God is not our Sugar Daddy in the Sky. He's not some cosmic Santa Claus looking for ways to make us more comfortable. He is looking for ways to make us more like Christ, so he wants to show how you respond when you don't get your way. Do you love him enough that when your husband isn't an Ephesians 5 husband, you can go on joyfully? Do you love God enough that when your job isn't all you wish it were, you can go on with joy, serving him, pleasing him, and putting in a good day's work at a job that your flesh hates?

Think about it. When do you grow the most—when you've got a husband who's just the way you want him? When do you become more like Christ, and cry out to him in desperate prayer as you search the Scriptures—when your whole world is ordered just the way you want it? No. It's when your husband isn't what you want him to be; it's when the job isn't what you had dreamed of, when your health fails, when your children rebel. That's when God meets you and conforms you to the image of his Son, Jesus Christ.

IDOLATRY FLIES IN THE FACE OF GOD

"You shall have no other gods before Me."—Exodus 20:3

Why is idolatry such a big deal? The short answer is that it flies in the face of God. In Matthew 22:37–38, Jesus quotes Deuteronomy 6:5: " 'You shall love the LORD your God with all your heart, with all your soul, and with all your mind.' This is the first and great commandment." In Exodus 20:3, God tells us that the number-one commandment is: "You shall have no other gods before Me." This is foundational.

Now let me give you the definition of an idol:

> *An idol is anything or anyone that captures our hearts, minds, and affections more than God.*

So what could be an idol in your life? Anything. That's why we're in such trouble, because absolutely anything can become an idol. Even a good thing, when wanted too much, becomes an idol. The Puritans called such things "inordinate desires." Idolatry is who or what you worship, what you long for, what your heart is set on. Idolatry is a big deal because it flies in the face of God.

IDOLATRY IS AT THE CENTER OF WHY WE SIN

> *"Therefore put to death your members which are on the earth: fornication, uncleanness, passion, evil desire, and covetousness, which is idolatry."*
> *—Colossians 3:5*

Idolatry is a big deal because it infiltrates and takes over the heart—the nerve center—determining the way we sin, when we sin, with whom we sin. Think of a bicycle wheel. The hub is the heart where the idols are. Each spoke is a specific sin, and you can trace each sin back to the hub—the heart.

In this war against sin, you must not be satisfied to simply stop sinning. As you work with your kids, with yourself, and with your spouse, identifying your heart's idols can help you to understand why you become so irritable, why you raise your voice. Identifying the idols of the heart is when the tide starts to turn. It's not enough to memorize some verses about anger and self-control. Go after the heart! There are heart issues behind all that anger. When someone is in a rage at home or in public, you can be sure that someone *else* has threatened one of his or her idols—and war is about to break out!

Anger, irritability, and verbal outbursts are indicative of heart issues gone awry. When you react to someone else, what is it that you are protecting? What is it that you must have? Husbands, doesn't the Bible say that our wives should respect us? Yes. But if you go around with the old "respect me" chip on your shoulder, constantly telling yourself, "My wife must respect me," you will inevitably be hypervigilant and hypersensitive; you will be perpetually angry, doggedly policing your wife's behavior, because for you, respect is not just something that God commands your wife to do, but something that you think you *must have* in order to be happy.

So many times, the conflicts that you're having can be traced back to your own desires, as we see in James 4:1–3. You think, "I must be respected," or "I must be . . . *whatever*," and it causes war between you and anyone who gets in the way of that desire. Then you cry out to God in prayer, and still don't receive because you ask amiss: "God, change her. God, you know I need respect. God, you know how important that is. Get her, God. You go." But God won't answer a prayer like that. He's more likely standing there with a two-by-four, wanting to smack you in the head and say, "Shut up and love her—stop worshiping yourself and thinking you are so important."

Our sin can be traced back to our idols every time. John Piper has summed it up this way: "Sin is what we do when we're not satisfied in God." Let me give you a corollary principle that you can use regarding idols. *Sin is what you do when you're chasing after something other than God, namely, one of your idols.* Idolatry is at center stage of my heart and your heart, because idolatry is nothing more than a metaphor for human craving, yearning, and greedy demands.

That's what we see in both Ephesians 5 and Colossians 3, where Paul is listing sins: "For this you know, that no fornicator, unclean person, nor covetous man . . ." and then he sticks this phrase in there: ". . . who is an idolater . . ." (Eph. 5:5). Paul connects covetousness and idolatry. We normally think, "Fornication . . . don't want to do that, but covetousness isn't such a big deal, is it?" But Ephesians 5:5 says "nor covetous man, who is an idolater . . ." When you're craving something other than God, even something good, God takes it very seriously. In that moment, he's coming after you. He's coming after you for his glory and your own good, because life for us is better without idols. Life for us is better when we're delighting in the gospel and loving Christ as our highest treasure. Life for us is better when we're focused on God and free from idols.

CHAPTER 2

IDOLATRY IS AN INSIDE JOB

IDOLATRY IS OUR NATURAL TENDENCY

No one has to be taught idolatry. We figure it out all by ourselves, and early on. No preschool has to offer training in this area as it does with colors, numbers, and Play-Doh. Kids figure it out on their own. Often, what you struggle with now concerning the idols of your heart began when you were a child, and you've spent the bulk of your life perfecting and protecting them.

God is calling us, by his Spirit and his grace, to stop perfecting and protecting idols, and rather to reject them. But oh, it's hard, not only because they don't want to leave, but also because we don't really want to lose them. Maybe the issue that you're struggling with and the idol behind it have been there for a long time, and you don't recognize them as enemies. Each one has become a friend, a companion that you're comfortable with, even a security blanket of sorts. You believe it's who you are and how you get through life.

Rejecting idolatry is hard. You don't drop your beloved security blanket in a heartbeat. It takes a work of God if you've been operating this way for a while. The temptation is to just make a slight modification—keep the idol but tweak it, just put a little Christian T-shirt on it. That's the danger: tweaking it rather than performing radical amputation and saying, "I can't keep living this way. This idol does not honor God, and it's hanging me up."

SO HOW DID YOU BECOME AN IDOLATER?

> *"Although they knew God, they did not glorify Him as God, nor were thankful, but became futile in their thoughts, and their foolish hearts were darkened . . . who exchanged the truth of God for the lie, and worshiped and served the creature rather than the Creator." —Romans 1:21, 25*

How does this happen? How do we become idolaters? We came into this world aware of a glorious God, aware of him through creation and conscience. Psalm 19:1 proclaims, "The heavens declare the glory of God; and the firmament shows His handiwork." We know it. It has been resonating in us for as long as we can remember—God is there. Look at the mountains, look at the oceans, look at your baby sister. God, God, God, God, God. Romans 1:19–20 says, "Because what may be known about God is"—what?—"manifest in them, for God has shown it to them. For since the creation of the world His invisible attributes are clearly seen, being understood by the things that are made, even His eternal power and Godhead, so that they are without excuse." We see it. We know it.

And then there's our conscience. Romans 2:15 explains that God put his law in our hearts, on our conscience, so we know there is a God. As he did for the Israelites in the Old

Testament, God has given us front-row seats to his glory and power. So why do we turn from God to the golden calf of idolatry? When we read Exodus, we think, "What's wrong with the Israelites? God had just led them through the Red Sea—parted the darn thing—wiped out the Egyptians, sent frogs and all kinds of other plagues against Pharaoh. God was on the move and on display, yet just a few weeks later, at the foot of Mount Sinai, they made a golden calf. What's with these people?" But we don't see it in our own lives. We don't remember the last good and glorious thing God did for us by the time the next trial hits. All we see is that moment—that trial—and we start making golden calves instead of trusting God.

Here's the struggle: Yes, God is glorious; yes, he's powerful. But he's not always on our timetable. That was the problem with the Israelites. They thought Moses had been gone too long. "He's not coming back," they said. "We have to take care of this ourselves." It's the same thing we struggle with now—timing. God's timing is not our timing. So we turn to something we *can* control, even though it serves us poorly. Our idols serve us so poorly; they hurt us, they cost us—but we think they're more predictable than God is, and they keep us in the driver's seat.

There's an unpredictability about God that we're not comfortable with. I don't mean to imply that, like us, he can't be counted on. Rather, God doesn't reveal himself to us so fully that we know exactly what he's going to do, how he's going to do it, every time and in every circumstance—and that drives us nuts. We know what God did the last time in a certain situation, so we assume that he'll do it that way every time. But it doesn't happen that way. And God doesn't send out memos, saying, "I see what just hit in your life, and I want you to know that I'm on it. Here's the timetable . . ." And so we turn to idols, often just to remove the uneasy feeling of waiting and depending on God.

God is good, but he's not safe. He will mess with your life—not just to be messing with it, but to conform you to the image of Christ. Yet the flesh wants to remove such uneasiness from your Christian walk, and idols offer a way to do it. But it's a lie, a false promise.

Because idols don't deliver.

That's what Romans 1:21ff. is talking about: "For although they knew God"—we start off knowing God—"they neither glorified him as God nor gave thanks to him, but their thinking became futile and their foolish hearts were darkened. Although they claimed to be wise, they became fools." Look at this: "and [they] exchanged the glory of the immortal God for images made to look like mortal man." Here's the great exchange: They exchanged the glory of God for the image of things in man, "the truth of God for a lie, and worshiped and served created things rather than the Creator" (Rom. 1:21–25 NIV). Anything that you exchange for God is a lie. It will not deliver on its promise.

For example, God gave us marriage. It is his gift, his design, his institution. But if you put all your eggs in that basket, thinking, "Marriage will provide all my peace, all my hope, all my love, all my joy," then you've doomed yourself to unending disappointment and heartache. Marriage can't bear such a burden. It wasn't designed to hold all that.

What about children? Aren't they a blessing from the Lord? Absolutely. But if you place all your hopes, all your expectation of joy and security, in those kids, you'll be miserable. Paul Tripp, in his book *Lost in the Middle*, says, "Children make terrible trophies."[1] Love them, enjoy them, train them, work with them, but don't make your children trophies, because you're setting yourself up for sorrow.

Richard Keyes writes:

> The natural human response to the true God after the Fall is rebellion and avoidance. Sin predisposes us to want to be independent of God, to be laws unto ourselves, to be autonomous, so that we can do what we want without bowing to His authority. At the most basic level, idols are what we make out of the evidence for God within ourselves and in the world—if we do not want to face the face of God Himself in His majesty and holiness. Rather than look to the Creator and have to deal with His lordship, we orient ourselves towards creations, where we can be more free to control and shape our lives in our desired directions.[2]

Now get this:

> However, since we were made to relate to God, but do not want to face Him, we forever inflate things in this world to religious proportions to fill the vacuum left by God's exclusion.[3]

We live in a culture that is forever inflating the things of this world to religious proportions, trying to fill the vacuum that's been left by excluding God. We see this phenomenon in sports, which in America has become one of the ugliest idols that we have to contend with. One spring, as the baseball season was cranking up, I saw a commercial showing clips of great baseball moments from the previous year. It ended with: "I live for this."

About that time, ESPN was running a series of commercials that asked, "What would we have to talk about if we didn't have sports?"

You see it with families—even Christians—driving their kids all over God's green earth, because "my child's really good. He's in a special league," which basically means that the family gets to miss church three out of four Sundays so that the kid can kick a ball, jump off a balance beam, or ride a horse. And that child, while being carted from one sporting event to the next in a cute little outfit, is thinking, "This is what it's all about. This is so important to Mom and Dad, what our entire home revolves around. I live for this."

I'm not saying that you can't be in a league or you can't play ball. But moms and dads, don't give in to the same spirit that the rest of our country has toward sports. As Christians—lovers of Jesus Christ—we have a higher calling. It breaks my heart to see Christians being sucked into the whirlpool like everyone else. I grieve when I see someone I've missed at church and say, "Wow, I've missed you guys," and they respond, "Well, you know, it's such-and-such season, and the kids are in a special league, and . . ."

Randy Patten, director of the National Association of Nouthetic Counselors (NANC), has a great principle: "Just add ten." Right now, she's eight years old, but just add ten years, and then you tell me where that eighteen-year-old girl will be on Sunday, after you've had her on the soccer field three out of four Sundays her entire life. Do you really believe she'll head back to church, thinking how important it is? If so, you're fooling yourself.

As soon as we drift away from Christ and the centrality of the gospel, we start erecting substitutes for God. That's why our culture is so desperate to make heroes and celebrities out of everything and everybody—because of our innate yearning for God and the freedom of his gospel, both of which we as a people have rejected. And we try to fill the void with hero and celebrity worship. G. K. Chesterton got it exactly right when he said, "When we cease to worship God, we do not worship nothing. We worship anything."[4]

HOW CAN YOU START TO DEAL WITH IDOLATRY IN YOUR OWN LIFE?

> *"Search me, O God, and know my heart;*
> *Try me, and know my anxieties;*
> *And see if there is any wicked way in me,*
> *And lead me in the way everlasting."*
> *—Psalm 139:23–24*

So how do you begin to deal with idolatry? Let me give you some homework. Get before God. At the end of this chapter is an exercise for you to work through. Take your time—don't just fill in the blanks. Get this personally, and apply it. As Jeremiah 17:9 ponders: "The heart is deceitful . . . and desperately wicked; who can know it?" God knows it, and will help you to know it. You don't have to be a master analyst or have the keenest insights or a degree in biblical counseling. Just be willing to say, with Psalm 139:23, "Search me, O God, and know my heart; try me, and know my anxieties."

And what are we so often anxious about? Our idols. We think, "What if I don't get what I want? What if I lose it?" Instead, we should pray, "Test me and see if there are any anxious thoughts in me and see if there are any offensive ways, and lead me in the way everlasting."

Don't do this just once. Do it three times. Not because God mumbles, but because we're such poor listeners. The first time, you won't get all that he wants to say to you. Sit down three times, alone and quiet with God, ten or fifteen minutes each time. Pray this prayer—Psalm 139:23—and say, "God, I want to know. I really do. Even if it hurts, I want to know. Show me the idols of my heart that are dishonoring you and leading me astray." And remember, your idol may not be some gross, obvious thing leering at you from the throne of your heart; in fact, for a believer, most often it's not. Usually it's something that we don't recognize in ourselves. We think we're doing the right thing for the right reasons, and we often have biblical references to back it up.

Counselor David Powlison gives this example:

> A woman commits adultery and repents. She and her husband rebuild the marriage, painstakingly, patiently. Eight months later, the man finds himself plagued with subtle suspiciousness. The wife senses it and feels a bit like she lives under FBI surveillance. The husband is grieved by his suspiciousness because he has no objective reasons for suspicion. "I've forgiven her. We've rebuilt our marriage. Communication is better than it ever was before. Why do I hold on to mistrust?" What finally emerges in the counseling is that he's willing to forgive the past but he's attempting to control the future.
>
> His craving could be stated this way: "I want to guarantee that betrayal never, ever happens again." The very intensity of his craving begins to poison the relationship. It places him in a stance of continually evaluating and judging his wife rather than loving her. What he wants cannot be guaranteed this side of heaven.[5]

I often have the unhappy privilege of telling people this. They want a biblical principle or a way that I can promise them that what happened will never happen again. There isn't one. We live in an unsafe, unpredictable world, but we have a very good and sovereign God, who is in control, who has a plan, and who cares for you. But there is no guarantee this side of heaven that whatever happened to you won't happen again.

Powlison continues: "He sees the point. He sees his inordinate desire to ensure the future but he bursts out, 'What's wrong with me wanting my wife to love me? What's wrong with me wanting my wife to stay faithful to our marriage?' " See how godly that sounds? That's where many of our idols are. They're cloaked in something that doesn't sound heinous at all. Powlison goes on, "Here is where this truth is so sweet. There's nothing wrong with the object of his desire. 'I want my wife to love me. I want my wife to stay faithful to our marriage.' There's everything wrong when it rules his life."[6]

FOCUS ON CHRIST AND THE GOSPEL

> *"I keep asking that the God of our Lord Jesus Christ, the glorious Father, may give you the Spirit of wisdom and revelation, so that you may know him better." —Ephesians 1:17* (NIV)

I want to end this chapter by leaving you with Christ. As you do the exercise, don't obsess over your heart while ignoring your Savior. Watch out! As you discover your idols, and God turns the floodlight onto the filth of your heart, you *will* be discouraged, so you'd better look to Christ! Read the Gospels again. Study the account of the cross. Go to Galatians and read about grace, not law. Preach the gospel to yourself every day. Delight in your Savior. Glance at your heart, but gaze at Christ. Keep the main thing the main thing.

Christ, the cross, the gospel—these are the main thing. So let whatever God chooses to do in your life be an occasion for you to draw nearer to your Savior than you have ever been, so that you'll be able to say, "That's why I need the gospel. That's why Christ died on the cross. That's why I need grace. That's why the law could never have saved me. Thank you, God, that according to Romans 8:1, 'There is therefore now no condemnation to those who are in Christ Jesus.' " Stay at the cross as God performs his surgery in you.

God, thank you so much for your Word. Thank you for its truthfulness. Thank you that, yes, it does cut, but you don't cut just to leave me bleeding. You cut to bring healing. You straighten what is crooked. You excise that tumor and that sickness, and then you pour in your healing balm of Gilead. Oh, God, cut me and then heal me, so that I might have more strength and vigor and passion and heart and freedom, so that I won't be dragging this wagonload of idols behind me as I try to go hard after you. I want to say "yes" to you, God, and "no" to idols—I want to love God and lose the idols. Help me, God, for your glory and my great, great good. I pray in Jesus' name. Amen.

IDENTIFYING PERSONAL IDOLS

Ask yourself:

1. Am I willing to sin to get this?
2. Am I willing to sin if I think I'm going to lose this?
3. Do I turn to this as a refuge and comfort instead of going to God?

More Questions to Ask Yourself as You Search Your Own Heart[7]

- What do you desire, seek, aim for, pursue, hope for?
- What are your goals, expectations, intentions?

- Do you want what *you want*, or do you want Christ's lordship over your life?
- Where do you look for security, meaning, happiness, fulfillment, joy, or comfort? Where do you put your basic trust?
- What would make you happy?
- What do you fear? What do you tend to worry about?
- What do you love and hate most of all?
- How do you define success or failure in a particular situation?
- What image do you have of who you are? Ought to be or want to be?
- If you were lying on your deathbed, what to you would sum up your life as having been worthwhile?
- What do you see as your "rights"?
- When you are pressured or tense, where do you turn?
- What do you pray for?

Personal Checklist

Place a ☑ next to the items/issues that you think might be current or potential idols in your life:

☐ Performance, especially for significant others: You try to please in order to get or to keep acceptance or approval. When you seek to please a person rather than God, this is idolatry. If this is the case, then you are worshiping that person rather than God, being fearful of what others think rather than obeying God.

☐ Performance of self (perfectionism): You try to perform to standards that you have set. When you meet the standard, you feel good; when you don't, you feel bad. You have made a personal list for yourself to follow that is higher than what God says. You're living like a Pharisee.

- ☐ Performance of others: You make a list of what others should do. Example: "For my spouse to be a good husband/wife, he/she *must* ____________." If your spouse doesn't do these things, you become judgmental and unloving.
- ☐ Good health: This shouldn't be your goal, except to glorify God. It's fine to pray for healing, but getting healed should not become your life's ambition or reason for living. God may want you to be sick in order to glorify himself (see John 9).
- ☐ Love of money: You take a promotion just to get more money.
- ☐ Success: What's a good day to you? What made it a good day in your mind? Usually it's along these lines: "I got a lot accomplished/done." Or "I pleased significant others." Or "I got my way. Others did for me what I wanted them to do."
- ☐ Fairness: Life has to be fair (Ps. 73)! "I've been trying to please God; others aren't even trying, yet they prosper." This can cause you to almost forsake the faith (Ps. 73:2).
- ☐ Hurt-free/pain-free life: "I don't want to deal with problems. There shouldn't be any difficulties. I shouldn't have to go through anything unsettling . . . because I just want peace."
- ☐ Christian marriage and home: "I want people to look at our marriage and think we have the best marriage in the world." Or "I cannot serve God and have joy until my spouse changes and starts doing _________." Or "I'll be successful if my children turn out right."
- ☐ Physical appearance.
- ☐ Being respected/admired.
- ☐ Being self-sufficient/independent.
- ☐ A material thing—for example, car, house, jewelry.
- ☐ Athletic abilities/achievements.
- ☐ Hobbies—sports, reading, whatever.

- ☐ An ideal—for example, pro-life movement, peace movement, political party.
- ☐ Success/position/power.
- ☐ Worldly pleasures—for example, drugs, alcohol, food, sex.
- ☐ Being in control.
- ☐ Meeting goals/achievements.
- ☐ A child or children.
- ☐ Getting married.
- ☐ Having your "needs" met.
- ☐ Other: ________________________________.

Now write the top five current or potential idols from your checklist onto this heart:

Chapter 3

Enough Is Never Enough

"You shall love the Lord *your God with all your heart, with all your soul, and with all your mind."*
—Matthew 22:37, quoting Deuteronomy 6:5

I said in chapter 1 that idolatry flies in the face of God. It violates the most rudimentary command, "You shall love the Lord your God with all your heart, with all your soul, and with all your mind" (Matt. 22:37, quoting Deut. 6:5). It also violates the very first of the Ten Commandments: "You shall have no other gods before Me" (Ex. 20:3). Idolatry is simply false worship.

Let's review our definition of idolatry: *An idol is anything or anyone that captures our hearts, minds, and affections more than God.*

So what could be an idol in your life? Here's the scary part: anything, even a good thing, can become an idol. For example, as I've served in the church, I've known ladies who would volunteer and work tirelessly at the church office. We'd all say, "What would we do without so-and-so?" But there can be a dark side to our serving. Could your serving become an idol? Could it be that you're serving not just the church and God, but also some personal purposes of your own, such as the desire to be needed and appreciated and recognized in ways that so often don't happen at home?

Could it be that you want to be well thought of, to have people say, "How did we ever get along without her?" But the woman who spends so much time volunteering at church might have a family who's saying, "Gee, we could use her help around here." Her husband feels that he's living without her. Laundry piles up, and he longs for a home-cooked meal, not to mention a romantic romp in the bedroom! Instead, his wife is always tired and seemingly unavailable. I'm not saying that if you're serving in the church, you need to quit. Just make sure that you're doing it for the right reasons, and make sure that your most important obligations—those to your family—are being fulfilled first.

I'm guilty of this very thing. In my own life, I have done things in ministry for the wrong reasons—and not only did my reasons need to change, but also some of what I was doing needed to stop altogether. It was simply too much. I could not play my guitar at every Sunday school event, lead every Christmas party, supply tracts at Halloween to every person who needed them, meet everyone who had a counseling need, prepare Sunday school lessons, visit hospitals, and still love my wife and kids the way I needed to.

Changing why I did what I did wasn't enough; I had to actually stop doing some of it. I wasn't cheating on my wife; I wasn't into pornography; I wasn't playing golf or hunting or fishing all the time. Everything I was doing was "God stuff." But guess what? Tucked inside God's kingdom was a mini-kingdom that served Brad Bigney. I had drifted from treasuring Christ and the gospel as first place in my life.

Nothing is harder than coming face-to-face with your idols and then putting them to death. You raise the knife to kill them and they roll, they squirm, they flinch. They're hard to pin down, and they seem to have a thousand lives. You think they're dead, but then they remake themselves and show up again. You have to have God's help if you're going to spot them, pin them down, and kill them as fast as they reappear.

Idolatry is false worship, living on substitutes; it's living your life with something other than God fueling your engine, and it doesn't work very well. You can drive your car with watered-down gasoline, but it will sputter and leave you on the side of the road a lot. Likewise, instead of recognizing our real problem, we try to create better substitutes that fail less often and with less severe consequences. But instead of finding better substitutes or more lifelike counterfeits, we need to repent of our idolatry and come back to the real thing—God. We need to come back to the Savior and the treasure of the gospel that set us free from all the idolatrous tentacles that keep wrapping around our hearts. We need to develop an unwavering eye for detecting and destroying idols as soon as they begin to creep in.

IDOLATRY IS ROOTED IN THE DESIRES OF YOUR HEART

> *"Put off, concerning your former conduct, the old man which grows corrupt according to the deceitful lusts." —Ephesians 4:22*

Stop looking outside yourself to find where idolatry is coming from. The main culprit is not an outside influence; it's your own heart. According to James 1:14, "each one is tempted when he is drawn away by his own desires and enticed." There's something residing in you—your own desires—that can draw you away. If someone claims to have a book or a sermon series that can show you how to kill those desires so that you'll never struggle with them again, don't buy it. The desires that James is talking about won't die until Christ returns or takes you home. The battle we fight is ongoing.

That's the battle that Paul wrote about in Romans 7:

> For what I am doing, I do not understand. For what I will to do, that I do not practice; but what I hate, that I do. . . . O wretched man that I am! Who will deliver me from this body of death? (Rom. 7:15, 24)

Then he goes on, in Romans 8, to praise God for Christ Jesus, who has given the death blow to that problem. But we're left to deal with its vestiges and leftovers. The death blow was dealt on the cross, but right now we live in the middle ground of the *already* and the *not yet*. God, by Christ's death on the cross, has broken the grip of sinful desires in our life, but we must still contend with our sinful flesh every day. The power and penalty of sin have been broken, but the presence of sin still remains.

David Powlison asserts, "Idolatry is by far the most frequently discussed problem in the Bible. The relevance of massive chunks of Scripture hangs on our understanding of idolatry."[1] How can that be true?

IDOLATRY IS NEVER SATISFIED

> *"Having lost all sensitivity, they have given themselves over to sensuality so as to indulge in every kind of impurity, with a continual lust for more."*
> *—Ephesians 4:19 (NIV)*

That little phrase—"a continual lust for more"—is what drives so much of the American economy. If not for that "continual lust for more," we'd all just buy a car and drive it until it died. It's that "continual lust for more" that keeps men and women sitting in front of slot machines, hoping to hear the jingle-jangle of coins. But when the cherries pop up, is the "lucky winner" going to shove those coins into his pocket and praise God? Will he thank God for his blessing, vowing to give half his winnings to missionaries? I don't think so! More likely, he'll head to the blackjack table and see whether he can double his winnings. He'll stay until he's lost it all, because there's something in us that the casinos have tapped into—a continual lust for more.

It's the continual lust for more that makes a person who already has more money than he knows what to do with invest a huge chunk of it in some get-rich-quick scheme, only to lose it all. It's the continual lust for more that makes a person respond to an email that says, "Dear Brother, I'm in Kenya and I want to give you a million dollars. I just need your bank account number and your Social Security number." And smart people, with real jobs, click "reply" and type in their information. Ephesians 4:19 tells us why this is: it's the continual lust for more.

And Ephesians 4:22 tells us that this lust is not only greedy but deceitful. It blinds us to common sense. It can drive a man who has a loving, beautiful, responsive wife to turn to prostitutes, homosexuality, bestiality, or some other sexual perversion. It's the continual lust for more. He forgets how good his marriage is and starts looking for something more. Many a woman today believes she needs to get a makeover, or to buy sexier clothing, when what she needs is for God to get hold of her husband so that he is content with what he has, rather than believing that whatever is across the line is better than what he has at home.

The continual lust for more is what drives a man to work sixty, seventy, eighty hours a week, trying to ride that corporate wave and be the flavor of the month, trying to land that six-figure salary, while the ones nearest to him are falling apart.

But the heart will never be satisfied apart from God in Christ Jesus. More of anything else in this life will never be enough.

It is impossible to live life effectively without God. He's the oxygen for life! Yet a man will strap on an oxygen tank and dive into life, trying to make it without God—but he keeps having to come up for air because the tank is limited, finite. And one by one the hoses on those tanks start to burst, and he ends up spending his life underwater, sucking air through a pinched hose and wondering why life isn't as good as he thought it would be. It's God that's missing. This man doesn't have the real thing! He's living on substitutes, and substitutes never satisfy.

But instead of realizing, "Oh, I've got a rubber hose in my mouth and a tank on my back. I wasn't meant to live like this," we tend to think, "I don't have the *right* tank . . . I'll try something else" or "I don't have enough tanks; there's somebody else who's got dozens of them. I just need more." And that's the lie. We need to come up, shed the tank, drop the rubber hoses, and breathe the fresh, wide-open air of God and God's grace. Only he can satisfy. Remember, sinning is what you do when you're not satisfied in God, and sinning is what you do when you're chasing after something other than God, namely, one of your idols.

GRASPING FOR THE WIND

> *"But when I looked, I saw nothing but smoke. Smoke and spitting into the wind. There was nothing to any of it. Nothing."—Ecclesiastes 2:11 (MSG)*

You can see this scenario played out in Ecclesiastes chapter 2. And what is so sobering is that we tend to think, "The only reason I haven't found satisfaction yet is that I haven't gotten as far down the path of pleasure as I'd like." But in Ecclesiastes chapter 2, you find someone who went all the way—someone whose wisdom can save you the heartache of running down the same path. He describes it as "vanity and grasping for the wind" (v. 26).

We live in a culture that loves testimonials; we pay attention to people's stories on *Dr. Phil* or Jay Leno. Well, here's the writer of Ecclesiastes telling us his story. In *The Message*, he puts it this way:

> I said to myself, "Let's go for it—experiment with pleasure, have a good time!" But there was nothing to it, nothing but smoke. What do I think of the fun-filled life? Insane! Inane! My verdict on the pursuit of happiness? Who needs it? With the help of a bottle of wine and all the wisdom I could muster, I tried my level best to penetrate the absurdity of life. I wanted to get a handle on anything useful we mortals might do during the years we spend on this earth.
>
> Oh, I did great things: built houses, planted vineyards, designed gardens and parks and planted a variety of fruit trees in them, made pools of water to irrigate the groves of trees. I bought slaves, male and female, who had children, giving me even more slaves; then I acquired large herds and flocks, larger than any before me in Jerusalem. (Eccl. 2:1–8)

Be careful as you read this lest you be unmoved, thinking, "I don't want flocks; I don't have slaves." What about houses? We can all relate to that, can't we? Who doesn't get excited about building a new house—designing, building, decorating? Maybe we don't design gardens or parks, but what about landscaping, making our yards beautiful? As for slaves, just substitute *dishwasher, stove, dryer*. That's what slaves did—they did your work for you. And the writer of Ecclesiastes "acquired large herds and flocks." He says, "I piled up silver and gold, loot from kings and kingdoms.

I gathered a chorus of singers to entertain me with song." Just substitute *Bose surround sound, great music, great sound system*. He continues, "And—most exquisite of all pleasures—voluptuous maidens for my bed. Oh, how I prospered!" (vv. 8–9 MSG).

He achieves what so many want—he beat everybody else. Much of the materialism in America is driven not by the thing itself, but by the desire to win—to beat somebody else. It's all about image, to attain what others don't. Our writer understands this. He says, "I left all my predecessors in Jerusalem far behind, left them behind in the dust" (v. 9 MSG). Now look at the irony in the next phrase: "What's more, I kept a clear head through it all." And we say back to him, "Sure, you did!" See how deceived he is? "I kept a clear head through it all. Everything I wanted I took—I never said no to myself. I gave in to every impulse, held back nothing. I sucked the marrow of pleasure out of every task—my reward to myself for a hard day's work! Then I took a good look at everything I'd done" (vv. 9–11 MSG). Slaves, gardens, pools, fruit trees, piled-up money, singers. "I . . . looked at all the sweat and hard work. But when I looked, I saw nothing but smoke. Smoke and spitting into the wind. There was nothing to any of it. Nothing" (v. 11 MSG).

It's the same today. Just look around the music, entertainment, and sports worlds. There's a slice of our culture that has supposedly arrived; they have everything that we chase so hard after, yet they're unhappy—they still want more. Magazines and television "shockumentaries" serve up a continual stream of celebrities whose lives have been destroyed by alcohol and drug abuse. Not long ago, I heard about a rap singer who's made more money than most of us can imagine, but he's checked himself into rehab, addicted to sleeping pills. With all that he has, there's one thing he still can't get: sleep.

Don't these celebrities have the stuff we just read about in Ecclesiastes? Yep.

We're tempted to think, "Yes, but that kind of life is excessive, flagrant, and sinful. I wouldn't do it like that. I'd handle it in a more toned-down, Christian kind of way. And I would tithe and help missions with it." Uh-huh. It's still lust.

Deceitful lust that just keeps wanting more.

IDOLATRY IS A SHALLOW SUBSTITUTE FOR CHRIST

> *"But the water that I shall give him will become in him a fountain of water springing up into everlasting life." —John 4:14*

Compare what we saw in Ephesians 4:19 and Ecclesiastes 2 with Scriptures that speak of the pleasures to be found in God. Lust is always deceitful, needing more, blind, deaf. The pleasures of God are abundant, overflowing, unending, forever. What a contrast!

Psalm 36:7–9 says:

> How precious is Your lovingkindness, O God!
> Therefore the children of men put their trust under the shadow
> of Your wings.
> They are abundantly satisfied with the fullness of Your house,
> And You give them drink from the river of Your pleasures.
> For with You is the fountain of life.

God doesn't just give you satisfaction. Rather than merely give you water, he establishes *in you* a fountain of living water.

That's why Jesus said in John 7:37–38, "If anyone thirsts, let him come to Me and drink. He who believes in Me, as the Scripture has said, out of his heart will flow rivers of living water." That's in reference to the Holy Spirit, who comes and lives in you. He sets up residence, makes his home in you, so that you have the source bubbling up inside you in unending measure, unlike the things of this world that people chase after. Idols never deliver this way. They just leave you with a nagging lust for more.

Imagine that you are adrift in a lifeboat in the middle of the ocean. Your tongue clings to the roof of your mouth, your throat is parched, and your lips are cracked and bleeding. You're dying for a drink of water while surrounded by it. The problem is, if you give in to that temptation, if you lean over the side of the boat and gulp down mouthfuls of that water, you will feel an immediate sense of relief and satisfaction that will be quickly followed by a ravaging thirst that is far worse than what you had before. *That's* what we're facing in our world today—especially here in America. It's as though we were in a boat surrounded by what looks like refreshing, thirst-quenching water, but it's full of salt. Everything outside of God in Christ is saltwater, and it only leaves you thirstier than you were before.

Remember how Jesus talked to the woman at the well in John 4? There she was, coming with her empty bucket, and Jesus knew that something besides her bucket was empty—her heart. She was looking for something she couldn't find, having been through five husbands, finally living with a man who was not her husband. But Jesus loved her, and knew she had not found what she was looking for. So instead of just drawing water for her, he said, "If you knew who I am, if you knew who was speaking to you, you'd ask me for a drink, and I would give you living water and you'd never thirst again." He wasn't talking about filling her bucket, which she could easily do herself. He was speaking of water that only he could give her, so that she would never thirst again. She surely knew, after five husbands, that men couldn't satisfy that need.

Jesus told her, "Whoever drinks of this water will thirst again, but whoever drinks of the water that I shall give him will never thirst. But the water that I shall give him will become in him a fountain of water springing up into everlasting life" (John 4:13–14). Christ alone has the thirst-quenching satisfaction that you've been looking for in all the wrong places. That marriage will never satisfy. That boyfriend or girlfriend will never satisfy. That facelift, that chat room, that job in the corner office—none of it will satisfy you long-term.

The day you tuck your legs under that mahogany desk and look out the window of your high-rise office, you will experience a sagging sense of "What now? I need more."

The day you get into that new car—the one you saved for, and longed for—and you take that first snort of leather and new-car smell, and you find out that it really will go from 0 to 60 in eight seconds, and you sail down the road with leaves swirling off the road behind you just as in the commercials—one day, sooner than you think, you will pull into your driveway with an oppressive sense of "That's it? I need more."

Young ladies, the day you tuck your shoulder under the arm of that guy you dreamed of, thinking, "If I ever got a guy like that, oh, honey, I'd be so happy," and you get a whiff of his horrible breath, or an encounter with his selfish attitude, the dream will quickly shatter—it won't satisfy.

I am not saying not to buy cars, not to live in houses, not to have relationships. Enjoy these things—but *don't live for them!* They cannot sustain you. You were made for something bigger, better, fuller. You were made with an appetite for God, and nothing else will satisfy.

So what about the stuff in Ecclesiastes chapter 2? Is it wrong to build houses, plant gardens, enjoy music? Not at all. First Timothy 6:17 says, "God . . . gives us richly all things to enjoy." So if you have them, enjoy them. Thank God for them. Just don't get lost in the gift and forget the Giver. Only God himself can satisfy.

IDOLATRY IS A THREAT TO YOUR SOUL

> *"Beloved, I beg you as sojourners and pilgrims, abstain from fleshly lusts which war against the soul." —1 Peter 2:11*

Idolatry doesn't just fly in the face of God; it's a threat to your very soul. First Peter 2:11 says, "I beg you as sojourners and pilgrims, abstain from fleshly lusts which war against the soul." It's a war. Maybe you have no peace, and your insides are churning, and you're praying, "God, give me peace. God, help." You read verses such as John 14:27, where Jesus said, "Peace I leave with you, My peace I give to you." You look at that verse, you remember Christ speaking to the waves, "Peace, be still!" (Mark 4:39), and you want that peace so badly for your own life, but it seems that God is not answering. Do you know what the trouble is?

So often when you're in the boat, and the storm hits, and the waves are crashing, you pray, "God, help me. Give me peace," but he's waiting for you to throw your idols overboard. You want God to send you peace while you hang on to them, while you row and live for something other than for him. But he won't do it. Don't think that God doesn't answer prayer. Don't say that he's not good. What he's doing is the very best thing for you—leaving you to rock in your boat with the storm blowing so that you'll wake up and realize that the idols have to go.

God doesn't give peace to people who are frantically clinging to, protecting, and perfecting their idols. He gives peace to those who reject them, then lift open hands to him and say, "God, rescue me, help me, deliver me! I'm done trying to make it happen. I'm done pursuing things that I think make up the 'good life.' I'm tearing up my list and laying it all down. God, come in and evict every usurper to the throne of my heart. Throw down every squirming, swarming idol that's smothering me so that I can't breathe, and come reign and rule in my life."

Now, that's a scary prayer. Because he just might put his finger on something and ask you to throw it out—something that you're not sure you can live without. Are you ready to say with the psalmist in Psalm 73:25, "Whom have I in heaven but You? And there is none upon earth that I desire besides You"? Let's be honest. We've never lived a single day when that verse has been fully true for us. Has there ever been a time when you could really say, "I desire nothing on earth besides you"? No—we desire all kinds of other things. What we need to say is: "God, make these verses true in my life: 'Whom have I in heaven but You? And there is none upon earth that I desire besides You. My flesh and my heart fail, but God is the strength of my heart and my portion forever.' "

The next verse tells how God comes against those who are drawn away to harlotry. Harlotry—prostitution, adultery—is one of God's favorite word pictures for how we chase after things other than him. And he doesn't promise to help us while we're doing it. Instead, he comes against us in our idolatry: "You have destroyed all those who desert You for harlotry" (Ps. 73:27).

IDOLATRY REQUIRES A SPECIFIC PLAN OF REPENTANCE

Idolatry is deep-seated in us, and won't let go easily. It will take more than a superficial housecleaning, so I hope you worked through the exercise at the end of the previous chapter and tried to identify your personal idols. That's a great start, but it's not the end. You can identify your personal idols, stick them in the back of your Bible, even put them on a mirror somewhere, but merely naming them won't make them go away. You have to take the next step.

Step two in this process is to put together a plan of repentance. Think about how you will repent in those areas. How will you change? And to do that, you'll have to think differently and live differently. List the idols you've identified, and then pray, "God, how should I think differently—how should I act differently?" Make a plan. I find that most people fail to change because they fail to make specific *plans* to change. Change doesn't just happen in "fuzzy land." You specifically sinned your way into where you are, and you're going to have to specifically repent your way out. Prayerfully think it through, and write some things down.

But before you jump into this exercise, I want to leave you with a quote from Ed Welch because I think he says it so well. Your focus should be on Christ: "The path of change goes through the heart and continues on to the gospel, where God most fully reveals to us his Son Jesus Christ in the death and resurrection of Christ."[2] Don't get bogged down in your heart with this change process that we're working through. Go through your heart—it may be dark and have some really discouraging spots, but continue on; go all the way to the gospel, and revel in it. Rejoice again that the gospel is your only power for real and lasting change, so that at the end of this book you can say, "Yes, I've learned more about my heart. And yes, I've repented, and I'm walking more closely with God." But to do that, grace has to taste sweeter, your Savior has to look better, and the cross has to loom larger over the landscape of your life—to the glory of God.

God, thank you so much for your Word. Lord, thank you that it is a sword that cuts and exposes me. Lord, thank you that in your other hand is a vessel of grace, so that as quickly as you cut, you're pouring on the grace. God, thank you. Cut me and give me your grace: grace to change, grace to see myself as you see me, grace to persevere—not just so that I'll have a better life, but so that I will be a trophy of grace that will honor you more fully, will be a more useful vessel in your hand, and will live breathing in the free, wide-open air, rather than spending my life submerged in the idolatrous substitutes, sucking on a hose with a tank on my back that the world has promised will satisfy. God, I'm throwing down the hose, unstrapping the tank, and coming back to you, and to you alone. I pray in Jesus' name. Amen.

Chapter 4

IDOLATRY WREAKS HAVOC IN YOUR RELATIONSHIPS

"For where envy and self-seeking exist, confusion and every evil thing are there." —*James 3:16*

Nothing but God will satisfy your heart, and yet your heart is prone to idolatry. That's the universal condition and universal dilemma, but by now I hope you've begun to take the concepts I've presented and apply them to your own life. What are the specific idols of your heart? Do you know yet? Maybe you're saying, "I don't want to know because I don't want to have to deal with it. I don't want to have to change. It sounds like a gut-wrenching experience and a bunch of hard work!" If that's what you're thinking, then at least you've been paying attention.

Most of the time, God has to show us our idols; we don't usually see them on our own. Think about it: if you knew what they were, you would have probably dealt with them before now. Have you been praying Psalm 139:23–24? "Search me, O God, and know my heart; try me, . . . and see if there is any wicked way in me." Have you written down what some of the main idols of your heart might be?

James 3:16 says, "For where envy and self-seeking exist, confusion and every evil thing are there." One of the places where chaos shows up most quickly and most painfully is in our relationships with those closest to us: husbands, wives, kids, parents, coworkers. They are the ones who bear the brunt of our idolatry, while we think they're only causing us trouble and getting in our way. They're frustrating us. They're blocking us. They're not helping us to get what we want. Have you ever felt this way or had any of these thoughts toward those around you, especially those closest to you?

CONFLICT EXPOSES OUR IDOLS

Paul Tripp writes:

> Do you have any conflict in your life? Do you experience moments of extreme irritation toward someone you otherwise love? Are there people who simply push your buttons more than others? Do certain things drive you crazy on a daily basis?. . . . Why does it seem that people, things, and situations are in our way? Why do we seldom go through a day without some experience of conflict? The answer to all of these questions is that we think of our lives as our own, and we are more committed to the purposes of our own kingdom than we are God's. We need to recognize that the people in our way have been sent to us by a wise and sovereign King. He never gets a wrong address and always chooses just the right moment to expose our hearts and realign them to his.[1]

Oh, how I wish I could tell you that this is not true, but it is. According to Scripture, God never gets a wrong address, and he always chooses the right moment to expose your heart—not just to afflict you or whip up on you, but to expose your heart, so that he can realign it to his. Until there is an exposure, there's no chance for realignment, but often that exposure takes place in the context of some painful conflict with another human being you're living in close contact with, so the process itself is anything but fun. And we never think it's a good time to have our hearts exposed and realigned. Our first reaction is often: "But God, this is the absolute worst time in the world for this to be happening. This new boss is coming down on me. This roommate is grating on my nerves. This new marriage is demanding far more of me than I expected. Don't you see everything else going on in my life? Not this—not now."

Yet we all smile and nod in small group or Sunday school whenever Romans 8:28 is quoted—as long as we're not the ones going through the trial right then. "Oh, yeah," we think, " 'And we know that all things work together for good to those who love God, to those who are the called according to His purpose,' but that shouldn't include this! Not this. Not here. Not now." We think, "There's no way this can work out for good. There's no way this came from God." We say, "God, you're not paying attention. This one slipped up on you. You've let things get out of hand."

But Ecclesiastes 7:14 says, "In the day of prosperity be joyful." We're good at that. But the verse continues, "But in the day of adversity consider: Surely God has appointed the one as well as the other." The conflict that you're facing right now with the people in your life is a divine appointment. That's right—it didn't just happen; it was on God's calendar.

GOD'S TIMING IS PERFECT

God never gets a wrong address, and he never chooses the wrong moment to expose your heart for the purpose of realigning it to his. It's like developing film. You take film into a darkroom and dunk it into some harsh chemical fluids. Then and only then do you begin to see the picture that was there all along. You didn't create a picture when you walked into that darkroom—you exposed one. You brought to the surface what was already on the film. And the same is true of your heart. So often it takes darkness, harshness, conflict, and pain to expose what was there all along. So don't run screaming from the conflict, saying that another person made you this or that. Don't look at your husband and say, "I was a loving mother until I had teenagers. Look what these kids have done to me!" Oh, no! The conflict with that other person is simply exposing what had been lying dormant in your heart all along.

Dave Harvey quotes John Bettler as saying:

> "Your spouse always hooks your idol." But marriage didn't simply hook my idols; it hoisted them six feet in the air and towed them around the house. I can't tell you how many times I thought, "I never had these problems before. This must be my wife's fault." The truth is, I'd always been a blameshifter—it's just that after getting married there were so many more good opportunities to express this fault![2]

The head-on collision with that other person is just flushing out the idols of your heart, stirring them up, sifting them out. That's good, and I don't say so lightly. Right now my wife and I are raising three teenagers, along with two other children, so there's a lot of flushing, sifting, and stirring going on. Sometimes it seems like we're in a constant whirlpool, as if our home is one big flush. But I've never grown this much spiritually in my life. And it's been ugly. I've been shocked at things that have come out of my mouth—things that I've been forced to trace back to my heart. It's been a wake-up call, a sledgehammer for self-deception, because we always think we're doing better than we really are.

But God loves us enough to pick the perfect time to smash our pious platitudes, to strip us of our self-righteous notions, and to leave us standing before him naked and embarrassed with our unruly idols.

OUR HEARTS NEED REGULAR REALIGNMENT

The heart is a tricky, slippery little creature that most often flies under the radar, giving us no reason to think about it. We live day after day, oblivious to the idols that are running up and down the aisles of our hearts, darting in and out of the clothes racks of our thoughts like wild hooligan children running loose in Walmart while their mother shops. And when we hear the occasional thuds that echo up from the recesses of our hearts, we tend to blame them on whatever or whoever is around us, until darkness or conflict sets in. And that's because we don't really see what's in our hearts until God takes us through some dark time, through some harsh trial that develops and exposes what was in our hearts all along.

My heart is just like my car. I'd love to take my car to the tire dealer for a lifetime alignment, so I'd never have to go back and pay for it again. But it doesn't work that way, because I drive my car. The minute I pull out of the parking lot, I begin undoing everything the mechanic has done: hitting potholes, running into curbs, not slowing down for speed bumps. You get the general idea. The wear and tear of everyday life makes a periodic front-end alignment necessary for a car, and it's no different with your heart.

I wish I could say, "During that Bible conference, or that revival service, or that one-on-one meeting with the Lord several years ago, I got my heart right with God, so now I can focus exclusively on other things." But we get jostled and bumped and slammed by life, and our hearts get out of alignment. The good news is that we don't have to remember to make an appointment with God to get it realigned. God chooses the right time, the right location, and even the right people to expose our hearts and to realign them to his. The conflict that we so often resent is God's appointment for a realignment of our hearts.

The problem is, we don't know that our hearts are out of alignment. We see only the conflict, the people, the rub. We're going through life, and our world is vibrating so much that it's hard to hang on to the steering wheel, and we're praying, "God, give me more grace, and *why are these people in my way*?" But God smiles and says, "Heart alignment is what you need. I'm going to keep those people right where they are, and we're going to get to work on your heart." We want him to remove the troublesome people and give us extra grace in their place, but he wants to realign our hearts to love him and other people more. The heart is what he wants to work on.

YOUR IDOLS HAVE DECLARED WAR ON EVERYONE ELSE

You're in a war every day, whether you know it or not. Every one of us is basically a dictator. Whatever the cost, you promote your own agenda and your own kingdom when idols rule your heart. Does that sound too ugly, too offensive? Am I overstating it?

James 4:1–3 says:

> Where do wars and fights come from among you? Do they not come from your desires for pleasure that war in your members?

> You lust and do not have. You murder and covet and cannot obtain. You fight and war. Yet you do not have because you do not ask. You ask and do not receive, because you ask amiss, that you may spend it on your pleasures.

But now move on to verses 4 and 5:

> Adulterers and adulteresses! Do you not know that friendship with the world is enmity with God? Whoever therefore wants to be a friend of the world makes himself an enemy of God. Or do you think that the Scripture says in vain, "The Spirit who dwells in us yearns jealously"?

God is a jealous God. He wants to rule in your heart, to be on that throne in place of all that other stuff. Likewise, James 4:6–7 says:

> But He gives more grace. Therefore He says [in Prov. 3:34], "God resists the proud, but gives grace to the humble."
>
> Therefore submit to God. Resist the devil and he will flee from you. Draw near to God and He will draw near to you. Cleanse your hands, you sinners; and purify your hearts, you double-minded.

Notice how God describes the heart: "double-minded." There's more than one thing that we are thinking and wanting. And that's what causes so much confusion and conflict, both with God and with other people in our lives. We're not focused solely on pleasing God and serving others. We are busy promoting our own agendas as well, and that makes us double-minded.

"Purify your hearts, you double-minded. Lament and mourn and weep! Let your laughter be turned to mourning and your joy to gloom. Humble yourselves in the sight of the Lord, and He will lift you up" (James 4:8–10). The problem isn't with your spouse or someone else. It's with your heart.

OUR IDOLS CAN DRESS UP LIKE GODLY VIRTUES

As a pastor, I found that one of the idols of my heart early in my marriage was: "I must be well thought of by the church." In other words, never say no. Always say, "Yes, I'll be there. I can do that. I'm your man." But with my family—my wife and kids—I was always saying, "We can do what we'd planned later. We have to change our plans. I know we had a date night scheduled, but we'll do it another time. It will happen." But it never did. It kept not happening because the demands and expectations of ministry continued to snowball as the church grew. I meant well—I really did intend to have a date night and a family night. It wasn't that I didn't want to be with my wife and family, but there was an idol on the throne of my heart that I was completely unaware of. And that idol of "I must be well thought of by the church" was driving me, though unconsciously, while I was convinced that what I was doing was right, and for the glory of God.

But I was deceived, and I was well on my way to destroying a wonderful marriage and home—not with alcohol or drug addiction, not with pornography, not with golfing, fishing, or watching sports all the time. Not at all—I was focused on the kingdom, baby. So you can imagine the arguments, *ad nauseam*, that we had with my saying to my wife, "Aren't you committed to the church and what God is doing?" But I was ignorant of my idols, and I didn't realize the ugliness of my own heart.

KINGDOM LINES BECOME BLURRED

The lines between God's kingdom and my kingdom had become blurred. What I thought I was doing with pure motives—and for the glory of God—was tainted with my own kingdom agenda of: "I must be well thought of by everyone at church."

It felt good to be loved by so many people at church. It felt good to be God's instrument again and again in the lives of so many people. But I did *so much* of it at the expense of my own marriage and family. While I was discipling and rescuing others, I was letting my own home wither on the vine. I was neglecting my God-given responsibility to love my wife the way Christ loved the church, and to train up and nurture my own children.

But ministry in your own home isn't as exciting, is it? It doesn't garner as many accolades. It doesn't turn heads the way public ministry does. But watch out. If you're not investing in your own marriage and family, it will turn heads eventually. What begins as a private failure will end up as a public humiliation, and it begins with your wife's countenance. The sorrow and sadness and neglect of a wife show up on her face long before the divorce papers show up in court.

But I wasn't the only idolater.

My sweet wife, Vicki, came into our marriage with her own idol: "I must have the perfect, godly family," a family that could be on the cover of *Focus on the Family* magazine one day. Every other woman will know that Vicki has so invested her life in her family, and has given herself away in such sacrificial service, that her husband and children rise up and call her blessed over and over and over. Only the blessed virgin Mary will have more accolades. I exaggerate, but you get the point.

Now imagine the conflict we had with these two competing idols, these two competing kingdoms. We were at war, and consequently never went long without a skirmish. At the same time we were confused, because neither us knew that an idol was ruling our hearts. No matter how much we talked, we could never find a resolution. We could never get our hands around the real issue.

The typical argument revolved around the latest incident of my canceling a family event to make room for yet another church activity. Or it would start with Vicki's saying, "I just feel like I haven't seen you." Either way the match was struck, the fire was lit, and we were off to the races with our umpteenth argument over time, church, ministry, and family life. I would pontificate about giving all for God, and how we needed to make sacrifices for the kingdom. But what I never said—because I was unaware of it—was that the sacrifice that I was calling us as a family to make also fed my own personal idol. It fanned the flame of what was most important to me. And so the sacrifice for me wasn't nearly as great as it was for my wife.

HOW DOES IT TURN INTO WAR?

What happened? How did it get to that point? When I stood at the altar on September 27, 1986, and said, "I do," I loved Vicki—I was committed to her. I wasn't aware of any malicious secret agenda that would one day shatter her dreams. I wasn't out to ruin her life—to see just how miserable a woman could be. But looking back, I see that my mind-set was one of: "Now I have a wife, and *together* we'll keep doing exactly what I was doing as a single man. Nothing will change. It's still my agenda, my kingdom—to the *glory of God*." I knew I was marrying a godly woman and believed she would just jump in and pursue my agenda with me.

I thought I had an incredible commitment to the gospel and to God's kingdom, but what I didn't know was how committed I was to my own personal idols. After Vicki and I became engaged, she had bridal showers and I had parties, but no one gave us an idolatry party, one in which our friends said, "Let's talk about idols. Let's bring all these idols out into the open. This will *really* help your marriage." No one helped us with that; no one talked about it. I was committed to Vicki; I was committed to God. But I was also unknowingly committed to my idols, to preserving and promoting and protecting them.

And also there with me on that September day stood a lovely young lady from Georgia, saying and meaning, "I love you, Brad Bigney. I'm committed to you, and I'm committed to God"—not realizing how committed she was to *her* idols.

The war that soon broke out between these two committed people was uglier than I could have imagined. We didn't hit each other or use profanity, but it was nevertheless hurtful and alienating and heartbreaking. We didn't know what was going on. I thought, "She's the problem," and she thought, "He's the problem," because two kingdoms were colliding—two thrones were crashing into each other. As we tried to promote our respective agendas, sparks flew, tears flowed, walls went up, and we entrenched ourselves more and more deeply in defensive positions.

We were disillusioned and confused. We were both Christians. We both loved Jesus. We had both graduated from Bible college. We both read our Bibles every day. So why couldn't we work this out?

YOUR IDOLS CHANGE THE WAY YOU SEE AND TREAT EVERYONE AROUND YOU

Having an idol is like putting on sunglasses. When an idol is what's most important to you, you will actually see life differently because of it. Idols skew your perspective. "These idols you've set up in your hearts cause you to stumble into iniquity" (Ezek. 14:3 paraphrase).

You can't see clearly with idols raging in your heart. James 4:1–3 connects our conflicts with other people to the internal war going on inside of us. Here's what happens: If my heart is being ruled by a certain idol, then there are only two ways I can respond to you. If you help me get what I want, help me promote my agenda—to move toward that idol, preserve it, protect it, enjoy it—then I'll be happy with you. We'll get along fine. I'll treat you well. I'll allow you into my world. But if you stand in my way, I'll be angry, frustrated, and testy when I'm with you. There will be times when I'll wish you weren't even in my life because you stand in the way of what I crave. I'll lash out at you. I'll push you away. I'll shut you out.

David Powlison says:

> I have yet to meet a couple locked in hostility (and the accompanying fear, self-pity, hurt, self-righteousness), who really understood and reckoned with their motives. James 4:1–3 teaches that cravings underlie conflicts. Why do you fight? It's not "because my wife/husband . . ."—it's because of something about *you*. Couples who see what rules them—cravings for affection, attention, power, vindication, control, comfort, a hassle-free life—can repent and find God's grace made real to them and then learn how to make peace.[3]

As a pastor, I see it often in marriage counseling. Usually, the breakthrough doesn't come because one spouse or the other gets it together and starts doing everything that the other person wants. It comes when one or both are broken before God and see the agenda they've been promoting and let it go—lay it down—and say, "God, you're enough. I'm going to focus on my part of the problem. I'm going to drink deeply at the well of Jesus Christ, and leave my spouse up to you. I'm going to focus on repenting of the idolatrous kingdom agenda in my own heart, the agenda that is the biggest reason our marriage is unraveling. I'm going to stop focusing on my spouse's problem, and start focusing on what you want me to see about me."

You can feel the tension leave the room when one spouse takes that first step.

Conversely, I've had to stop counseling with more than one couple who make no progress, even after months and months of counseling, because they're entrenched in their respective corners, protecting and promoting their respective kingdom agendas, each hoping the other will lay down arms and wave the white flag. They strangle the life out of their marriage while they grip their little agendas, refusing to humble themselves, each afraid of coming out on the short end of the stick.

Elyse Fitzpatrick and Jim Newheiser get it right:

> Let us challenge you to do something that we've tried to do as we've faced our family difficulties: strive to win the gospel race! Think to yourself: If I'm the first to confess, the first to repent and humble myself, the first to the cross, I'll experience renewed grace from Him! I won't have to worry about trying to defend my own reputation or the "moral high ground." Instead, I'll be flooded with God's mercy. Remembering that God resists the proud but gives grace to the humble (1 Peter 5:5) should motivate you to resist the temptations to blame, to hide, and to win.[4]

It should also motivate us to let go of our idols and to repent of the logjam of competing agendas that's sucking the life out of our relationship.

Listen—whenever you repent of the idols of your heart, you're the winner. You get God's grace, God's favor, God's blessing, and God's power.

CRAVINGS UNDERLIE CONFLICT

Many times when I finish up counseling with couples, it is obvious how much better they're doing. They touch each other during the sessions. They smile. They make eye contact. Their relationship is back to the way it's supposed to be—not perfect, of course, but better. The hostility and coolness are gone. And sometimes one of them—usually out of earshot of the other—will say to me, "You know what? My spouse really hasn't changed that much. But I've changed what I expect, what I think, and what I crave, and that's made all the difference."

Very often also, the other person will change far more, and far more quickly, without an idol-gripping spouse who screams for change or else withdraws with self-pity and manipulation and pouty little games.

How about you? Is this what your marriage desperately needs? Let me save you some money. You don't need a tummy tuck or a longer vacation together. You don't need a book on sex technique. What most couples need in order to transform their marriages is to repent of the idols of their hearts. Cravings underlie our conflicts. What are you craving? Look at your relationships and ask, "Where am I having conflict?" The two are not unrelated. Cravings underlie conflicts.

YOUR IDOLS HIJACK LEGITIMATE DESIRES AND TURN THEM INTO UGLY DEMANDS

So is it wrong to have desires? Is it wrong to desire a godly marriage? Is it wrong to desire kids who grow up to honor God and make you proud? Of course not.

But idolatry hijacks legitimate desires and turns them into ugly demands. Paul Tripp, in his excellent book *Instruments in the Redeemer's Hands,* unpacks the way in which our idolatrous lusts wreak havoc in the lives of others around us. The diagram below typifies what so often happens in our relationships.[5]

Affects my relationship to other people

Desire ➡	**Demand** ➡	**Need** ➡	**Expectation** ➡	**Disappointment**
"I Wish" Morphs into	"I Will!"	"I Must"	"You Should!"	"You Didn't . . ."

Spirals down into . . .

⬇

"Because you didn't, now I will . . ."

or "Because you didn't, now I won't . . ."

Legitimate Desires Turn into Demands

Let's walk through it. An idol starts off as a desire. Okay, nothing wrong with that. It sounds like this: "I'd like to have a godly marriage." Or: "I wish my husband were more attentive to me, more nurturing and affectionate." Or: "It sure would be nice if the kids would . . ." These are legitimate desires. Try this: Picture a desire as being held in an open hand. A demand is a desire that you begin to white-knuckle and clutch in your little clenched fist. It is no longer "I wish . . ." or "It sure would be nice if . . ." It becomes: "I *must.* I must have kids who . . . I can't live without . . . I must have a spouse who . . . I must have the kind of boss who . . ."

We Relabel It a **Need**

That's when it gets ugly, and it reminds us of a kid in his high chair, banging his little fists. Our culture has helped us down this road with psychology that encourages us to progress from desire to: "I *need* this . . . Oh, if you understood my background and all that I've been through and the brokenness in my home and how dysfunctional we were growing up, you would agree that I need a husband who is attentive. My love tank is dry. I can't function without that. I can't go on the way things are." It's not just a desire, it's not just a demand; it becomes a *need*.

Expectations Kick In

Once you start calling something that you want your spouse or your kids to do a *need*, your expectations immediately kick in. After all, if something is a need, then the people closest to you—who say they love you—ought to help you to get it, right? And once expectations kick in, get ready to be disappointed, because that person you expect to meet your needs is a sinner. If you're expecting your needs to be met by anyone other than God, then you just put your expectations in a sinner.

For example, people put these expectations on a spouse and end up getting deeply disappointed, hurt, and broken. And when the marriage ends, they simply start over with someone else, hoping that this person will meet their needs. It's the same in any relationship, whether with a spouse, a boss, a roommate, or anyone else. What people don't realize is that they're just moving their "needs" from one sinner to another.

Disappointment Leads to Punishing Each Other

Disappointment awaits you if your expectation is fixed on anyone other than God. And once disappointment sets in, it quickly spirals into punishment. You'll begin operating under a system that thinks but doesn't say something like this: "You say you love me. Here are my needs." Then: "You're not meeting my needs, so I'm going to punish you . . . I'll leave . . . I won't have sex with you anymore . . . I won't pick up your dry cleaning . . . I won't serve you in any way . . ." You begin to punish each other because you're disappointed that the other person didn't meet your expectations.

This is what concerns me about the content of so many marriage and relationship books today. I'd like to wrap yellow caution tape around so many of the best-selling Christian books out there that focus on the husband's needs and the wife's needs. Think about it—just because a husband knows his wife's top five needs doesn't mean that he'll have any desire to meet them. Why? Because he's too busy thinking about *his* top five needs, hoping that she reads the chapters on how she can meet his needs. This approach leaves both of them focused on themselves and striving to get the other to meet these so-called needs.

These books should be titled *His Desires/Her Desires*, subtitled *Your Spouse Will Never Meet Your Desires, So Shut Up and Get Over It and Get to Know God.*

That may sound harsh, but it would be far more helpful, because what these best-selling books have done is to describe what your spouse's top needs are, so that now there is no excuse for not meeting them. You can't say that you don't know. At least before reading the book together you could assume the best and think, "Well, he doesn't know what I need." Now you can't say that. Now you say, "We did the study together. He knows my top five needs. These are things I need as a woman." Meanwhile, he says, "These are things I need as a man." So now you're both really hurt and really mad, because your spouse is still not meeting your needs.

Both husband and wife could be helped far more by studying God and what it means to die to self, rather than studying their top needs that really aren't needs, but desires clutched in a closed fist.

God, thank you for the hope in Christ. Thank you for Jesus Christ, his work on the cross, his grace, and his blood. Lord, I pray that you would reveal to me the idols of my heart so that I might repent of them, so that I can love the Lord my God with all my heart and soul and mind and strength, and so that I can love my neighbor as myself. Lord, my idolatry causes me to use people and love things. God, help me to repent so that I can love people and pass grace on to them. I ask in Jesus' name. Amen.

A TESTIMONY OF THIRTY YEARS OF HEARTACHE

If you think I'm just crying "wolf," and you're not convinced that idols of our hearts end up hurting the ones we love most, then listen to the story of a woman in our church who spent more than thirty of her fifty years trying to move forward in life, while picking through the shrapnel of her mother's idolatry that wreaked havoc in her home as she was growing up. And notice how it continued to spill over into her own home after she was married. She says:

> Mom had several idols, and in her defense I'm sure some of them started out being rather admirable. But as her life went on, her desires became demands, and then needs, and then expectations. And when those expectations were not met, the disappointment came like a flood. And all her friends and everybody in her family were punished.
>
> God's Word is clear when it says, "You must not bow down to them or worship them, for I, the Lord your God, am a jealous God who will not tolerate your affection for any other gods. I lay the sins of the parents upon their children; the entire family is affected—even children in the third and fourth generations of those who reject me. But I lavish unfailing love for a thousand generations on those who love me and obey my commands" (Deut. 5:9–10 NLT).
>
> In retrospect, one of the idols that I saw in Mom's life was status. Once that took root, other idols began to be incorpo-

rated. To a great extent, her son (my brother) became an idol, in that he would help her attain a goal of being important.

On February 14, just a few years ago, my mom passed into eternity. When Dad called me the afternoon of the 15th, he said, "Hello," and began to cry. I knew immediately that Mom had died. His words summed up everything, and showed me that even in death, Mom would still try to control him. He said, "I called because our pastor said I should." Mom had kept my dad from communicating with me for years, and even in death Mom wanted to keep control, and to keep Dad from having a relationship with me. And even though she was dead, he was still scared to go against her, for fear that she would still be able to punish him somehow.

So what would make a woman so bitter and angry? What had I done? How had I disappointed her? Well, in 1944 Mom met and fell in love with a young carpenter who worked for her father on the railroad. Her father always spoke highly of this young man, and when he brought him home for dinner, it didn't take long for the two of them to fall in love. After he returned from World War II, they were married, and three years later my brother was born. But there were problems. He was born with a mild case of spina bifida and only part of one ear.

At this point, when his spine fused and he was able to function normally, and with plastic surgery to restore his ear, my mother's life began to revolve around her son. Life was all about Chip, and as we were growing up, Mom always talked about Chip's becoming a doctor. And when she talked about it, she would always stress that people would see her as important then. Conversations would sound like this: "People will know who I am because my son is a doctor. That will teach them a lesson. They won't be inclined to look down their noses at me. I'll show them." This was so often the tone of so many conversations in our home.

Mom also started to bemoan the fact that she was married to a poor carpenter, who didn't make much money and hadn't finished high school. She was constantly correcting Dad's grammar and putting him down. Now, keep in mind that all of this was going on while Mom looked like the picture of a godly woman on the outside. She was very involved in the church and community, using many of her talents and gifts. She often played the role of hostess for many Saturday-night gatherings in our home.

So what went wrong? Well, if you pursue your idols long enough, you reach a point where you turn a corner, you change, and not for the better. Recently my oldest daughter and I were looking through a family photo album, when she suddenly pulled out two pictures and gave me a puzzled look. Then she pointed out how my mom's countenance had completely changed from one photo to the next. One picture was taken while I was in the seventh grade. The other was taken a year later. And my daughter was right. Mom looked happy in the first picture, but the second one showed an angry, bitter person. Mom had turned her corner in that year, and it got even uglier.

That next year, as an eighth grader, I watched our family really begin to fall apart. Chip went away to college and enrolled in pre-med on a campus where Mom had gone to great lengths to get him. It was a college of status for her, so that she would look important. But as I look back, here is where Chip's life began to unravel. He began to drink and smoke heavily, and eventually he said he was on the verge of a nervous breakdown and dropped out of college altogether. No doubt he couldn't take the pressure of fulfilling Mom's dream of gaining status through him.

Mom didn't take this lightly, and her life really started to unravel. During this time, she began having problems of her own, which were magnified by her desire for all the attention to be focused on her. She was instructed by her doctor to go home after work, have a glass of wine, and relax. But soon after, she became an alcoholic.

During my years in high school, Dad's brothers and sisters were all facing difficult times, and they turned to him for help. My parents and I were making lots of trips to the hospital. I never really thought much about it. Dad's family needed help, and so we were there to help. But Mom's blood was beginning to boil. One Valentine's Day, Mom and Dad were headed out to dinner. My uncle stopped them at the end of the street and asked them if they would mind taking his brother-in-law's glasses to him at the hospital. What followed should never have happened. Mom went over the edge and exploded.

Now, you haven't lived until you've experienced my mother's wrath, and that's what came down on Dad that night. By the time the dust settled, Mom had cut off all contact with Dad's side of the family. Now, I'm sure there were things they did that added to the problem. But nothing that deserved being cut off for the next thirty years. Yes, thirty years.

By now Mom was known in the church and in the community as an angry, nasty person. She was mad because, as she saw it, people at church didn't appreciate her for all she did. She was turning on her friends and didn't seem to have anything nice to say about anyone. It was as though everyone she associated with had suddenly become ignorant, and she had no use for them. Meanwhile, Chip's life was falling apart. He had moved to North Carolina, where he'd married, picked back up with his university studies but once again failed, and continued drinking and smoking heavily.

With Chip in North Carolina, I was stuck living with a wrathful mom, and a dad who would not buck her on anything. Her drinking magnified her anger, and her bitterness spilled out on everyone she came in contact with. I had chosen a college-prep path in high school, but one day my mom went to the high school and changed my program without my knowing it. She informed my guidance counselor that I was to get into fashion merchandising. I was now going to be a famous designer and make her look great. So you can imagine what she thought when, in my senior year, after feeling God's call on my life, I announced that not only was I going to go to college, but I also wanted to go into church work. Sounds like an admirable plan, but since Mom's dream of getting me into commercial art didn't come true, and her son had already failed to make her important, when I announced my plan to go into church work it all hit the fan.

Now, you need to understand that in my town and in our family, girls were not supposed to go to college. It wasn't even supposed to be an option for me. So Mom spent the next several hours that night calling the relatives that she was still speaking to and telling them the awful thing that I had done. And I can still vividly see her face and hear her screaming, "What have I done to deserve this? Oh, my God!"

Since Mom didn't get her way with me, she again turned back to my brother and his wife.

Every chance she had, Mom would say something to incite an argument between Chip and his wife. Now, you would think that a thousand miles between Chip and Mom would be enough distance, and that of course Chip would defend his wife. But that didn't happen. As Mom looked for ways to undermine Chip's marriage and attack his wife, Chip sided with Mom. His marriage fell apart, and he missed out on so much with his son, Andrew. Eventually Chip moved back home with Mom and Dad and never moved out. Even as a grandmother she was nasty, and none of her grandchildren had any respect for her.

Almost ten years ago I called my mom and confronted her on two minor issues—just two. I wasn't mean or spiteful in my approach, but her response was predictable, and it went like this: "I don't need you. I don't want you. We don't need you. And we don't want you." Then she proceeded to scream at my dad and then Chip to hang up. That was the last conversation I had with Chip. He died of liver cancer three years later. The pastor at my parents' church let me know by email that Chip was dying, and when I asked him whether he thought Mom would allow me to visit my brother, his response was: "I don't want to hurt you any more than you've already been hurt. Your mother would not let you in the house if you showed up at the door. She hates you. But keep in mind, it goes way beyond you. You became the target of her wrath when it really doesn't have anything to do with you." He also shared with me how people in the church could see how nasty she'd become in life.

When Chip died, the pastor contacted me, saying he thought Chip's death had broken Mom enough that she was ready to hear from me. Wrong. As I walked into the funeral home, I stopped and watched my parents for a moment as they stood at Chip's coffin. And I simply prayed, "God, here's where you're going to have to take over, because I want to wring her neck. So it's going to have to be all of you and none of me." After the funeral, as I was getting out of the limo, Mom said, "Let's make like none of this has ever happened." Oh, that was Mom. "Let's push it under the carpet and pretend nothing happened." She obviously didn't think she could be wrong.

For the next several months, I tried to keep an open door and called home each week. But as time went on, nothing changed. Mom was still demanding that life revolve around her. I won't even go into all the nonsense she pulled over the next several months, so that after Christmas I finally stopped trying to communicate with her.

In spite of all I had gone through, I still had a love for my dad. My prayers over the past nine years were that somehow I would get my dad back. I missed my dad. Even though he never stood up to Mom as he should have, I understood his fear of her. He didn't believe in divorce, and he knew what she would do if he confronted her. So he chose to live with it.

So when Dad called last February, I knew Mom was gone. I also knew that Mom didn't want Dad to call me and tell me that she was gone. I could just hear her: "Don't you call her. We don't need her."

Mom didn't get the status she demanded, or so many of the other things in life that she felt she deserved, or the career she wanted. Her son, who was supposed to be someone great, died an alcoholic and on welfare. He failed at college, at his jobs, at his marriage, and as a father. He died a failure.

And Mom missed out on enjoying her children and grandchildren. She was always afraid of death and never wanted to die alone, but that's exactly how she died. All her self-made idols crumbled, leaving her an angry, hateful, bitter woman. All but two of Dad's brothers and sisters had died before they could even reconcile. Out of fear of and submission to my mother, for thirty years he'd had no contact with them.

Since Mom's death, Dad has made contact with his remaining brother and sister. And it's been such a joy to watch the relationships grow, and to hear how happy the three of them are. His sister (my aunt) is 104, and for thirty years she's wondered what she did to incur such treatment. But now she knows the truth. The grandchildren have met their uncle and aunt for the very first time. My husband has finally met them. Until this past summer, my husband had never met anyone on my dad's side of the family. No one.

Now my dad struggles, trying to figure out what went wrong with Chip's life. And living with Mom for almost fifty-nine years certainly left scars. But with God's help, I've been able to piece some things together for Dad, and I'm helping him to heal. As for Mom, well, Jonah 2:8 puts it so well: "Those who cling to worthless idols forfeit the grace that could be theirs" (NIV).

Now, you might read that account and think, "Well, Brad, that's extreme. You went out and found the worst example you could find. It's not always going to be that bad!" Please notice that this story didn't begin with sins that looked horrific, but look at how it ended, and look at the irreversible impact on three generations of a family. Idols multiply. It's not worth it. Wherever you are today, check out the craving that underlies conflict, and repent. Don't let it grow. Don't let it fester. Don't let it spread through the family.

First, for the glory of God, and second, so that you can be free to love your neighbor as yourself.

Chapter 5

Idolatry Changes Your Identity

I want you to see the extent of the battle we're facing as we study this issue of idols of the heart, and why it's so hard to repent. This is an age-old battle. Our struggle is nothing new. You see it spelled out in Romans 1:21–23:

> Although they knew God, they did not glorify Him as God, nor were thankful, but became futile in their thoughts, and their foolish hearts were darkened. Professing to be wise, they became fools, and changed the glory of the incorruptible God into an image made like corruptible man—and birds and four-footed animals and creeping things.

Just because we don't live on the Amazon and worship the sun or the moon, don't think we're not idolaters as much as the people Paul described were. They might exchange God's glory for a four-footed animal, but we exchange it for a husband, a child, a job, a vehicle, a house, an idea, a fit body, prestige, or whatever. We are all idolaters, all over the globe. We differ only in how we manifest our idolatry.

Our passage continues:

> Therefore God also gave them up to uncleanness, in the lusts of their hearts, to dishonor their bodies among themselves, who exchanged the truth of God for the lie, and worshiped and served the creature rather than the Creator, who is blessed forever. Amen. (Rom. 1:24–25)

Notice that the phrase is not "for *a* lie," but "for *the* lie." You know what the big lie is? That you can live on something other than God, that you can make it on something other than God, that you can find happiness and peace and meaning and purpose with something other than God.

One reason that the battle against idolatry is so fierce, and that idolatry is so hard to shake, is that you're not just clinging to substitutes for God. You're not just standing there with a handful of counterfeits. The problem is much bigger, and it's rooted far deeper.

IDOLATRY CHANGES HOW YOU SEE YOURSELF

When you're snared in the trap of idolatry, you take on an entirely different identity. You start redefining yourself in light of that particular idol. Now, not only do you live for your marriage or your kids, you so define yourself by your idol that you *become* your marriage or your kids. That's why, when one of those things you live for is threatened, you react so fiercely and violently. You are struck with panic if it's taken away, or if someone gets in the way of that thing, because it's not just a thing or a person you enjoy; it's *who you are.* There's a loss of self. You're afraid that you're going to lose yourself.

You take on false identity in light of your particular idol, so to even think of turning away is like turning away from yourself, losing yourself, having the rug pulled out from under you. It creates a sense of disorientation. If you're still struggling, wanting to repent and put this into practice in your life, you need to realize that the identity rock you're standing on may need to crumble underneath your feet—and that's a completely life-altering idea.

Paul Tripp says that we are *identity amnesiacs.* And when you suffer with identity amnesia, it always leads to identity replacement. Whenever you stop rooting your identity in who you are in Christ, you replace it with something else.

Tripp writes in his book *Lost in the Middle* that we take on experiences, relationships, or accomplishments as our identity: "Sinners tend to move away from defining themselves in relationship to their Creator and begin defining themselves in relationship to the creation. But the creation cannot bear the weight of defining us. It will always come up short. It is bound to happen, and when it does, a moment of disappointment can quickly turn into a fundamental loss of self."[1]

What should be a moment of disappointment becomes a fundamental loss of self. When psychology talks about someone's needing time or space to find himself, it usually means that the person's identity was wrapped up in something or someone that was never designed to sustain him. So this crisis he's having is a good thing. The problem is that he's probably in secular counseling, and he's not being told, "Your identity, your rock, your substance, your reason for living, the reason God put you here, is to be in relationship with your Creator." Many times, the person is just given a new substitute to replace the old one.

False Identity Takes Place Unconsciously

I don't know anybody who wakes up one day and says, "I'm going to set my heart on this person or this thing, and I'm going to let it completely control my life." But that's what happens, subtly, gradually:

> The person you met and mildly enjoyed becomes the person whose approval you cannot live without. The work you undertook to support your family becomes the source of identity and achievement you can't give up. The house you built for the shelter and comfort of your family becomes a temple for the worship of possessions. A rightful attention to your own needs morphs into a self-absorbed existence. Ministry has become more of an opportunity to seek power and approval than a life in the service of God. The things we set our hearts on never remain under our control. Instead, they capture, control, and enslave us. This is the danger of earth-bound treasure.[2]

SET YOUR HEART ON GOD

Now, here's the good thing: set your heart on God. He's definitely not under your control and never will be. But the effect of setting your heart on God is that it makes you a very free person. You're free from other people. You're free from running the rat race and living like everyone else in the world. It frees you and fulfills you. But when you set your heart on other things, some earthbound treasure, whether it's in a body, a person, or a substance, it begins to enslave and control you. That's why Proverbs 4:23 says, "Keep your heart"—to what extent?—"with all diligence, for out of it spring the issues of life."

According to 2 Chronicles 16:9, "the eyes of the LORD run to and fro throughout the whole earth, to show Himself strong on behalf of those whose heart is loyal to Him." Set your heart completely on God, and you get his help and support. Today God is looking for a certain kind of person, and you could be that person. Today you can't instantly lose fifty pounds, or grow more hair, or become vice president of a company. I'm giving you a promise that you could enjoy today. The eyes of the Lord *today* are moving to and fro throughout the earth, looking for this kind of person, the one whose heart is fully his, and God will support that person.

Common Identity Replacements That Result from Idolatry

One of the most common identity replacements is "I am my success." You define yourself in terms of achievements. Do you want to be good at what you do? Absolutely. Being a Christian doesn't mean you're so humble that you want to do a sorry job at work in order to be the last one recognized. "God will be pleased by that," you say. "I'm just very humble." No. You should work hard because Christians should work hard. It ought to be that business owners say, "Let me find a Christian to hire. They work hard whether the boss is looking or not, because they do it as unto the Lord."

Living for God's Glory Slips into Living for Your Own

But if you live for the praise, the recognition, the "atta boys," you've crossed the line from working for the glory of God to idolatry, and it will ensnare you. You know that God is loving, that he's gracious, he's merciful, he's kind, he's patient—but he's also jealous. And he will come and upset that little apple cart of yours if he sees that you're no longer working excellently for the glory of God, but for the glory of yourself.

God is worthy of having it all be about him, and he knows you are most miserable when you live for anything other than him. So the most loving thing he can do is to rise up in his jealous, righteous anger for his own glory and your good, and topple the house of cards you've built for yourself, because you won't find lasting fulfillment and peace in living that way. Isaiah 42:8 proclaims, "I am the LORD, that is My name; and My glory I will not give to another, nor My praise to carved images."

"I am my success." This is the profile of a workaholic who gets his meaning from the next notch on his belt, so that he finds it almost impossible to say "No" or "Slow down" at work. It's the woman who doesn't just enjoy playing tennis or soccer or softball—she lives for it. This is the person who wakes up every day, motivated by one thing—getting that next promotion. The title on the office door defines the person, not just the job.

WHEN WHAT YOU DO BECOMES WHO YOU ARE, YOU'LL FEEL THREATENED BY OTHERS

I hope you're not already ensnared in "I am my success." But I also hope this helps you to better recognize what's going on when you collide with people in the workplace and get a violent reaction. You're bumping into their identity. You're a threat to them. You get that lashing out, backstabbing, and character assassination, and you think, "What have I done?" You've threatened their idol. You've threatened their kingdom. You've threatened their very existence and identity.

If a newer or younger person with greater abilities comes into the company, you feel threatened, displaced. Or maybe your batting average on the softball team defines who you are now. It's far more than recreation; it's identity. If you take your identity from your job, or from sports, or from something else, it won't be long until you start seeing the ordinary demands of a spouse and family as getting in your way. You'll start to resent time being taken away from your business or hobby because *that* has become your identity; it's what you live for. And bitterness and envy sprout when you see people around you who are divorced or single, and since they're free from family responsibilities, they can pour themselves into that job or hobby.

I felt that as a young pastor. There I was, in my late twenties, living in a trailer with a wife and three children, while all the other pastors on staff were older and had already raised their kids. But there I was, with an idol of "this ministry is who I am, this is my identity, and I want to do it to the glory of God," but I think "to the glory of Brad" was really what was going on. And there those other pastors were, coming in so early and staying so late. And as I gathered my stuff to leave at normal times, it was so hard because I was thinking, "They're still in the office. They're still working. Look at me. What are they going to think about me? How will I ever live up to that?"

Now I gather my stuff and leave when I ought to leave, even if the other pastors are still working. I can say, "God, I answer to you. It's not about appearances now. It's not a competition. I want to work hard for the glory of God, and you know what and how much I'm doing, and you know I have five kids and other responsibilities." But you can do that only after those idols die, not while they're raging in your heart. Achievement was never meant to give us identity. So when it replaces our true biblical identity, it leaves a harvest of bad fruit.

What about you? Does personal achievement mean more to you than it should? I know it's a hard question. I know you're sitting there thinking, "I don't know. I mean, am I just a hard worker or . . . ?" Take it before the Lord. Ask him, "Does personal achievement mean more to me than it should? Is there idolatry at play here? Is it really for the glory of God? Is that all that's going on here?"

KEEPING THE GOSPEL CENTRAL FREES YOU FROM DEFENDING YOURSELF

Could it be that you've been looking to success as the source of your identity, meaning, and purpose? Learn something from the apostle Paul here. In Philippians 1, Paul was in jail. That will really slow you down in this whole climb-the-corporate-ladder thing. Others were out there planting churches, evangelizing, building their ministries. He was in jail. And what you find in Philippians 1 is the ugliness of competition, even in ministry and the spread of the gospel. Paul says in verse 15, "Some indeed preach Christ even from envy and strife."

Do people go out and preach Christ in a competitive way? Do churches go so far as to hate each other, even though they're all Christians and all going to heaven? Yes, and it's not a new thing. Look at this: "Some indeed preach Christ even from envy and strife, and some also from goodwill: The former preach Christ from selfish ambition, not sincerely, supposing to add affliction to my chains" (Phil. 1:15–16). Paul is saying, "I'm already sitting in jail chained up, and they think this will hurt me even more as they get ahead of me." The NIV says that these people "stir up trouble for me" (v. 17). They're not just preaching the gospel; they want to make trouble for Paul.

But Paul's identity is in Christ. He's not wrapped up in claiming, "I am an apostle. I am a church planter. That's my whole identity." He understands that he is a child of God. Jesus died for him; God rescued and forgave him. Paul's greatest treasure is not preaching the gospel; it is owning the gospel for himself, delighting in the fact that God chose him, saved him, and keeps him for his glory. Paul hasn't forgotten that he was a murderer, snorting threats and on his way to throw more Christians in jail when God knocked him off his horse and saved him. Paul knows that this is the most important identifying thing about him, not any church he has planted, not any inspired letters he's written, not the gospel he has preached. Therefore, this man could say, "What then? Only that in every way, whether in pretense or in truth, Christ is preached; and in this I rejoice, yes, and will rejoice" (Phil. 1:18).

Now, *there* is a man who knows who he is in Christ. There's a man who has fought hard to distinguish "I'm a child of God" from "Oh, by the way, he's called me to minister full time as an evangelist and apostle." And you don't have to be in full-time ministry for these verses to apply to you. You are a child of God first, before whatever else you do. After that, you're a wife, a husband, a worker, a softball player.

DON'T LOSE SIGHT OF WHY GOD IS USING YOU

Another fellow in Scripture who understood this truth was John the Baptist, who wasn't threatened when the ministry of Jesus began to overshadow his own ministry. That sort of thing hurts, doesn't it? Now replace the word *ministry* with your job, your skills, your gifts. Suppose someone comes along and begins to overshadow you, so that you're no longer the flavor of the month.

But John the Baptist understood who he was—he was solid on his identity. And when his role began to fade in the glory of Christ's arrival, he didn't spiral into depression. He didn't fearfully cling to his role. He didn't lash out at those who were leaving him for Christ. Look at John 3:26, and you can see the mentality of John's disciples, who ran to him and said, "Hey, Rabbi, someone else is getting more attention than you. Your followers are leaving us and going after Jesus now." There was John the Baptist, sent by God to prepare the way for the Messiah, to announce that Christ was coming; and when he did come, John's disciples were so caught up in John's ministry that they were actually afraid—threatened—when in fact everything was going according to plan.

John's ministry was *supposed* to be temporary, serving only to point to Christ. And when it started happening, John's disciples felt threatened and said, "Rabbi, He who was with you beyond the Jordan, to whom you have testified—behold, He is baptizing, and all are coming to Him!" (John 3:26). I can just picture John saying, "And the problem is . . . ?" Then "John answered and said, 'A man can receive nothing unless it has been given to him from heaven' " (v. 27). He understood who he was, and that the work he had done wasn't his to begin with. Who you are and what you're doing isn't yours to begin with—however good you are at it, however God is using you, it was given to you. And if God chooses to take it away, he can do so to his glory and for your good.

John the Baptist told his disciples, "A man can receive nothing unless it has been given to him from heaven. You yourselves bear me witness, that I said, 'I am not the Christ,' but, 'I have been sent before Him.' He who has the bride is the bridegroom; but the friend of the bridegroom, who stands and hears him, rejoices greatly because of the bridegroom's voice. Therefore this joy of mine is fulfilled" (John 3:27–29). He had to make it very basic for them: "You feel threatened. You feel anxious and panicky. I'm filled with joy because this was supposed to happen." He summed it up this way in John 3:30: "He must increase, but I must decrease."

Paul and John the Baptist understood and faced the counterfeit identity of "I am my success." You need to do the same.

"I AM MY RELATIONSHIPS": DEFINING YOURSELF BY THE PEOPLE AROUND YOU

With this particular counterfeit, you define yourself in terms of the people around you. You don't just enjoy people; you don't just love them or serve them; you need them to serve *you*. This is where it gets dicey—God is a God of relationships. He designed us to live in community with one another. He models the importance of relationship in the Trinity itself—God the Father, God the Son, God the Holy Spirit—throughout all eternity, fellowshipping with and relating to each other. This is one thing that sets man apart as being in God's image. He's a relational God. We are relational beings. We want to be in relationship with other people. But our sinful, idol-making hearts take it a step further, searching for other people to do for us what they were never designed to do: give us identity, purpose, and meaning.

You'll Start Using People Rather than Loving Them

It's great to love people. It's great to enjoy and serve them, to appreciate the camaraderie of social interaction. But with relationships, you're always on a slippery slope; and it's easy to slip, so that what started out as loving other people, to the glory of God, suddenly becomes craving their acceptance and affirmation for your own glory. Rather than finding your security in God's love, rather than standing on the rock of Christ, you stop loving other people, and instead use them to fill the void in your life that only God can fill.

You start craving the attention, affirmation, or laughter of other people. You have to have it, and you despise anyone in small group, at work, or on the softball team, who gets it, because they are a threat to your little kingdom. You wish they weren't there because they're getting what you crave, what you want, what you have to have. At that point, you are an approval junkie, using people rather than serving and loving them to the glory of God. And once you head down that path, the "performance for significant others" idol takes over, and your life becomes nothing more than a dog-and-pony show, with you hoarding the spotlight, vying for the approval of those around you.

Second Corinthians 5:9 cuts through all that: "Therefore we make it our aim . . ." What are you supposed to be doing? What should your sights be set on? "Therefore we make it our aim, whether present or absent, to be well pleasing to Him." So many people spend so much energy and time trying to please people, yet make no effort at all to please the one person they're supposed to please—God.

So many people struggle with the idol of "performance for significant others" that pop psychologists have given it a name. The label they use is *codependency*—living for, and being tied to, the approval of another person in your life. But it's been around forever, or at least as long as two sinners have lived in the same place at the same time. The Bible has a much more accurate term for it: *man-pleaser*. It's not just a psychological thing that the Bible doesn't address. You don't need to go anywhere else to find help for it.

Saul

In 1 Samuel 15, King Saul chose to please his people rather than God. God had told him to slaughter all the Amalekites and all their animals. But Saul wanted to please his people, so he kept the animals alive and spared Agag, the Amalekite king. Then when Samuel the prophet showed up, Saul started running his mouth, saying something like this: "Oh, bless you. It's so wonderful to be serving God together, and I've done everything in the Lord."

Samuel replied, "Be quiet and let me tell you what the Lord told me last night." And brace yourself—this was not a little deal. If you think it's not such a big deal to live your life to please people rather than doing what God says, listen to the consequences of Saul's disobeying God, choosing instead to please the people. God said, "I'm taking the kingdom away from you. I'm going to give it to somebody who will obey me."

First Samuel 15:22 says, "To obey is better than sacrifice." But Saul wanted the approval of the people.

Pilate

Mark 15:15 informs us: "So Pilate, wanting to gratify the crowd, released Barabbas to them; and he delivered Jesus, after he had scourged Him, to be crucified." Pilate knew that Jesus was an innocent man. His wife had had a dream the night before, and told him, "Don't have anything to do with this." And he thought washing his hands ceremonially in a bowl of water was saying: "Okay, I'm done with this. It's not my responsibility anymore." Yet he was the one in authority. The buck stopped with him. But wanting to please the crowd, he turned Jesus over to be crucified.

Peter

In the book of Acts, God gave Peter a marvelous illustration to show that there was no longer any distinction between Jews and Gentiles—the wall had been torn down, and people were all equal at the foot of the cross; salvation was through Christ for everybody. There was no longer the clean and the unclean. God showed Peter unclean animals and said, "Kill and eat" (Acts 10:13). But Peter replied, "Lord, I've never done that." God told him, "Don't call anything unclean that you can eat with thanksgiving as unto the Lord."

And before long, Peter was hanging out and eating with Gentile believers, which according to Old Testament law was a big no-no. Along came a group of Judaizers, bigwig religious leaders. And Peter pulled away from the Gentiles. Maybe you'd say, "Oh, that's just a little thing." But it wasn't a little thing. And Paul rebuked Peter to his face and said, "How can you do this? How can you be such a poor example, wanting to please mere men?"

HOW THIS FALSE IDENTITY AFFECTS YOUR PARENTING

So how would this idol of "I am my relationships" show up in your life? Paul Tripp gives an example in the area of parenting: "Joanna thought she had grown in her faith. The problem was that she had forgotten who she was, and it was not long before her identity in Christ was replaced by another identity. Joanna's children became her new identity."[3]

Moms, my heart goes out to you. I understand how this happens, because you give so much. Kids are so needy. You've got to wipe them, and spank them, and talk to them, and hold them, and dress them, and protect them, and on and on . . . it starts to feel like that is all you do. I understand that it's hard. Don't quit doing those things, but fight hard to be reading your Bible enough, and worshiping enough, and thinking straight enough to say, "I know this is taking all I've got, but it's not who I am." You will find yourself spiraling into a horrible pit of depression if you don't keep that distinction.

Tripp goes on to say that when Joanna's children became her new identity, they really did give her meaning and purpose, they really did give her hope and joy—for a while. The problem was that they weren't designed by God to do any of that. Joanna lived vicariously through them, and the more she did, the more she became obsessed with their success.

> She remained faithful in her personal devotions and public worship, but God was no longer at the center of who she was.
>
> And it didn't take much for little Jimmy to mess it all up. With all his inner turmoil, Jimmy made a poor trophy. Being with him often spelled unexpected confrontations and public embarrassment. Forced to live in the shadow of Jimmy's drama, Joanna's daughters turned out to be poor trophy children too.
>
> When her children left the nest, Joanna was lost, paralyzed by what had happened to them, not just because she loved them so much, but more importantly because of what their struggle had taken out of her. In their tumultuous launch into adulthood, the kids not only broke Joanna's heart, but also robbed her of her identity. She felt like it had all been for naught. When she looked in the mirror, she felt she didn't know the person she saw there anymore.[4]

Many times it takes a painful trial to expose idolatry.

REMEMBER WHO YOU ARE IN CHRIST!

Proverbs 29:25 says, "The fear of man brings a snare, but whoever trusts in the LORD shall be safe." So what is the solution to identity replacement? Remember who you are in Christ. Who you are in Christ has to define your identity, and you need to be constantly reminded of this. That's what Bible reading is all about. Don't fall into the trap of thinking that the Bible is just an index for problems (I'm struggling with anger—show me some anger verses; I'm struggling with pride—show me some pride verses). Do you know what the Christian's number-one problem is? Identity amnesia—forgetting who you are. The Bible reminds you of who you are in Christ.

Think about how many times Scripture writers, especially of the Epistles, launch into who you are, not just "do this, and don't do that." Colossians 3:1–2 teaches, "If then *you were raised with Christ*, seek those things which are above, where Christ is, sitting at the right hand of God. Set your mind on things above, not on things on the earth."

Peter's second letter is all about knowing who you are:

> Grace and peace be multiplied to you in the knowledge of God and of Jesus our Lord, as His divine power has given to us all things that pertain to life and godliness, through the knowledge of Him who called us by glory and virtue, by which have been given to us exceedingly great and precious promises, that through these you may be partakers of the divine nature, having escaped the corruption that is in the world through lust. (2 Peter 1:2–4)

Now, after telling us who we are, he's going to tell us some things to do. But watch how, as he does this, he comes right back around to who you are:

> But also for this very reason, giving all diligence, add to your faith virtue, to virtue knowledge, to knowledge self-control,

> to self-control perseverance, to perseverance godliness, to godliness brotherly kindness, and to brotherly kindness love. For if these things are yours and abound, you will be neither barren nor unfruitful in the knowledge of our Lord Jesus Christ. For he who lacks these things is shortsighted, even to blindness, and has forgotten that he was cleansed from his old sins. (1:5–9)

That's why we need to sing about forgiveness, about redemption, about full atonement. We need to be reminded to keep the main thing the main thing.

Second Peter 1:10–11 says, "Therefore, brethren, be even more diligent to make your call and election sure, for if you do these things you will never stumble; for so an entrance will be supplied to you abundantly into the everlasting kingdom of our Lord and Savior Jesus Christ."

Now watch how many times he uses forms of the word *remind*:

> For this reason I will not be negligent to *remind* you always of these things, though you know and are established in the present truth. Yes, I think it is right, as long as I am in this tent [this body], to stir you up by *reminding* you, knowing that shortly I must put off my tent, just as our Lord Jesus Christ showed me. Moreover I will be careful to ensure that you always have a *reminder* of these things after my decease. (2 Peter 1:12–15)

Your idolatry is bigger than just clinging to a few counterfeits. It includes taking on an identity replacement that leads to a sense of losing yourself. Find your identity in Christ and Christ alone. Stand on the rock of what Christ has given you—your salvation, your redemption, your forgiveness, your clear conscience. If you don't know Christ, you can't even begin to do the things you have just read about. I urge you to come to Christ; find your identity in him. Receive forgiveness today. Call out, and experience that mercy. If you know him, repent of how you've begun to live for and take on the identity of anything other than Christ.

Part 2

SO WHAT'S THE SOLUTION?

Chapter 6

We Need an X-Ray of the Heart

"Where do wars and fights come from among you? Do they not come from your desires for pleasure that war in your members? You lust and do not have. You murder and covet and cannot obtain. You fight and war. Yet you do not have because you do not ask. You ask and do not receive, because you ask amiss, that you may spend it on your pleasures."—James 4:1–3

Your Idols Are Rooted in Your Heart

". . . in their hearts."—Ezekiel 14:3

Let's dig a little deeper into this topic. Where do idols come from? How do we get into trouble in this area? We're going to spend time in Ezekiel chapter 14 because I want to show you some verses that I think give the best explanation of what's going on inside of us. It's like having an X-ray made. A few years ago, I snapped the ACL in my left knee at youth camp, but all I knew was that I'd never felt pain quite like this before. On the way to the hospital, I was thinking, "Why is there such a screaming pain in the side of my leg? What in the world is hurting so badly? What have I done?" But when the doctor clipped the X-ray of my knee up on the light board and began to explain, it all made sense: "Here's what you've done . . . Here's what we see . . . Here's what we understand . . ."

Ezekiel 14 is like that. The difference is that it is not a medical student or even a seasoned surgeon speaking to you. It is your Creator. He has clipped an X-ray of your heart to the light board and says, "Let me explain to you why your life's going the way it's going, and why there's so much pain.

"Your problem is idols of the heart."

Heart idols lie behind so many of our specific sins. So many of the ongoing struggles we have with other people and so much of our anger, fear, and depression can be traced back to idols in our heart. That's why Proverbs 4:23 warns, "Guard your heart above all else, for it determines the course of your life" (NLT). In other words, as the heart goes, so go your dreams, your emotions, your choices, your priorities, your life. It all starts in your heart.

For example, someone might have a serious anger problem, but he won't begin to see victory until he recognizes and understands that he has a serious idol—a ruling idol—such as "I must be respected," or "I must be well thought of." And when he's not respected or well thought of, he responds in anger. Anger is simply his response, his retaliation, for not getting the respect or admiration he desires. The battle becomes much clearer and he begins to see progress when he targets his idols, rather than just memorizing four or five "do not get angry" verses.

You have to go after the heart.

Jeremiah 17:9 says, "The heart is deceitful above all things, and desperately wicked; who can know it?" But Ezekiel chapter 14 shows

Jeremiah 17:10 in action: "I, the LORD, search the heart, I test the mind, even to give every man according to his ways, according to the fruit of his doings." We don't know our hearts, but God does. He says, "I search the heart; I test the mind. I'll clip it up on the light board, and I'll show you what's going on in your life—why you sin, the way you sin, with whom you sin, when you sin, how often you sin, and why that particular sin is so hard to shake."

What I find in my own life is that if I'm having a hard time shaking a particular sin, a herd of idols is almost always associated with it. That's what makes it so hard to get rid of. That herd of idols fuels and feeds that sin, and drags you back to it again and again.

Ezekiel 14:1–8 relates:

> Now some of the elders of Israel came to me and sat before me. And the word of the LORD came to me, saying, "Son of man, these men have set up their idols in their hearts, and put before them that which causes them to stumble into iniquity. Should I let Myself be inquired of at all by them? Therefore speak to them, and say to them, 'Thus says the Lord GOD: "Everyone of the house of Israel who sets up his idols in his heart, and puts before him what causes him to stumble into iniquity, and then comes to the prophet, I the LORD will answer him who comes, according to the multitude of his idols, that I may seize the house of Israel by their heart, because they are all estranged from Me by their idols."'
>
> "Therefore say to the house of Israel, 'Thus says the Lord GOD: "Repent, turn away from your idols, and turn your faces away from all your abominations. For anyone of the house of Israel, or of the strangers who dwell in Israel, who separates himself from Me and sets up his idols in his heart and puts before him what causes him to stumble into iniquity, then comes to a prophet to inquire of him concerning Me, I the

> Lord will answer him by Myself. I will set My face against that man . . .' " "

Things are not looking good here. God is saying, "Yes, you come to me—you pray, you cry out. Do you want to know why life is so hard? I'll tell you, and I'm not going to talk about the specific hurt that you want me to remove. I'm going to talk to you about one thing and one thing only—your idols." Ezekiel 14:8 continues, "I will set My face against that man and make him a sign and a proverb, and I will cut him off from the midst of My people. Then you shall know that I am the Lord."

Let me ask you some questions as we work our way through this passage. This may be the first time you've ever stopped to unpack Ezekiel 14:1–8, let alone tried to apply it to your life. Let's get all the good that we can out of it.

YOU'RE THE ONE WHO PUT THEM THERE

> *"Son of man, these men have set up their idols in their hearts." —Ezekiel 14:3*

Where are these idols that are causing so much trouble? "In their hearts." How did they get there? "These men have set up their idols in their hearts." So who's to blame for the trouble? "These men" are.

You say, "I'm not aware of that happening. I don't know that I've done that." God says, "These men have set up their idols in their hearts." Do you think we're any different? No, we're to blame for our idols—not Satan, not our mamas, not the neighborhood, not Hollywood, not even the government. We did it. It's our fault—and not only is it our fault, it's our very nature. It's our very nature to be idol-makers.

You're the one who put your idols there. You say, "I'm not setting up idols in my heart. Wouldn't I know it if I were doing that?" Let me put it this way: do you ever have thoughts about wanting something that is outside the bounds of God's principles, precepts, and commands?

For instance, maybe you're unmarried, and whether you're a teenager or a single adult, you might want to have sex with your boyfriend or girlfriend. You wonder if it's really so wrong to sleep together right now, even though you're not married. You begin thinking, "If we really care about each other, it's not wrong. If we're two consenting adults, it's not wrong. If we practice responsible, safe sex, it's not wrong." Maybe you begin thinking, "I deserve intimacy and pleasure and satisfaction. My life is so hard. I'm lonely. God is a God of love, right? He doesn't want me to be unhappy. I would have more joy—I'd be a better testimony, a better witness for him—if I weren't so lonely."

"And," you say, "God made me a sexual being. He wouldn't want me to deny that aspect of myself, would he?" I'm not saying to deny that you are a sexual being—sex is a gift from God. I'm only suggesting that you delay the gratification of that gift. *Delay* and *deny* are not the same thing. Know that your loving Creator knows best.

We have an uncanny ability to reason our way into sin, to excuse choices and lifestyles that we know flatly contradict God's commands. Is anything like that going on in your heart and mind right now?

Maybe you fantasize about that guy at the office, thinking, "He really understands me, he listens to me, he looks me in the eye when I'm talking, he doesn't interrupt. He's so gentle and caring—unlike my husband."

Or maybe you have the opportunity to take a little money on the side at work, so you tell yourself, "They don't pay me enough. Besides, I do the work of two people—so padding my expense account is still saving them money."

Do you see what's going on?

You're setting up idols in your heart, putting something before God, his Word, his precepts. Remember our definition of an idol: *An idol is anything or anyone that begins to capture our hearts, minds, and affections more than God.* It's living on substitutes, exchanging the one true living God for a counterfeit, and we do it all the time.

Draw the bull's-eye on yourself; don't blame Satan. It's you, it's me. We're the biggest problem. Raise your hand and say, "It's me!"

Satan uses all the material we give him to work with. He sees better than we do what's coming out of our hearts. He's not omniscient, nor can he read our minds. But after thousands of years of practice, he is an expert at reading people, at reading *you*—what you say, where you look, your responses, your body language. James 1:14 doesn't read, "Each one is tempted when he is drawn away by Satan." It says, "Each one is tempted when he is drawn away by *his own desires*."

Let me illustrate it this way. An expert fly fisherman isn't just born. He learns from the old-timers; maybe he takes a class or studies books on fly-tying and fly-fishing. However he goes about it, he doesn't stop until he completely understands the colors, the texture, and the feathers that work best for making a fly that will attract the biggest brown trout in the stream. Satan also studies, but he studies to know the textures, colors, and stimulants that work best to hook us into sin. He goes to school on our individual idols. He studies, he observes, he listens. Then he fashions the specific lure for you or for me.

But Satan's strategies would never work if our hearts were not already teeming with idols. He simply casts the lure out there that matches the idol of our heart. It hits the water, and then up from the depths of that heart lunges the trophy-sized trout of desire, which immediately chomps down on the lure. Then all Satan has to do is to set the hook and reel us in.

In his book *Lost in the Middle*, Paul Tripp explains:

> The Bible exposes us for who we really are. Scripture never allows us to believe in a neutral, undirected, or unmotivated humanity. It requires us to admit that behind everything we do or say, we are pursuing *something*—some hope or dream or thing that we refuse to live without. These are things we value so much that we will willingly sacrifice other good things to get them. We will debase our humanity in order to deify the creation. The very things we seek to possess begin to possess us. We live for shadow glories and forget the only Glory that is worth living for. In its masterful portraiture of humanity, the Bible requires us to make one painfully humbling admission—the one confession we work so hard to avoid: *that our deepest, most pervasive, most abiding problem is us!* If you can humbly make this admission, your life will never be the same.[1]

But it's so hard to admit that, isn't it? We want the problem to be someone else, and we want it to be solved by someone else, so that we won't have to deal with it. But it's us; we're the problem. And yes, it's fed and fueled and exacerbated by the world around us, and it's exploited by the devil. But we can't blame the world. And we can't say that the devil made us do it.

Yes, Satan is an enemy. Yes, we need to pray against him. Yes, we need to be on guard against him. But if we go through life with the mind-set that Satan is the biggest reason we sin, we won't see the victory we can gain by thinking, "I have an enemy who is an expert at tempting me, but I need to fight right here, inside myself. I need to repent of the idols that are raging in my heart, so that the devil won't have so much to work with."

Satan simply works with the material that we give him.

YOUR IDOLS KEEP YOU FROM SEEING AND AVOIDING SIN

". . . causes them to stumble into iniquity."
—Ezekiel 14:3

What is the end result of idols in your heart? They cause you "to stumble into iniquity." Your idols become stumbling blocks. Do you ever wonder why it seems that you just fall into sin? We even talk about it that way; when a pastor runs off with a woman in the choir, we say, "He fell." And that's the way it seems, because nobody saw it coming. For years, you hear him preach his heart out, and you think he's doing fine—then, seemingly without warning, he falls.

Ezekiel 14:3 teaches that the idols of your heart cause you to "stumble into iniquity." That pastor didn't one day decide, "I'm going to wreck my marriage and bring dishonor to the name of Christ." But there were specific idols that he had been serving. He had been telling himself, "My wife just doesn't appreciate all I do . . . she doesn't give me the affirmation I need . . . but this woman on the praise team—every time we get together, she tells me what a great pastor I am, what a great dad I am. My wife never tells me that." This lady's comments fed this idol of his: "I have to have encouragement. I need affirmation."

Was he thinking, "I want to commit adultery"? No, but his idol was getting fed and getting fat, and when it got big enough he stumbled into iniquity. Idols cause you to stumble into sin.

You have to think about what you're thinking.

Life is demanding. Every day we have a thousand things competing for our attention, and that's what most of our thinking is consumed with. But we rarely stop to think, "What is going on in my heart?"

Underneath all the frantic busyness of day-to-day living, you're thinking something. For instance, you may find that being around a certain person—at work, in a meeting, at church—leaves you with a jittery, high-school kind of feeling, like the wind of love blowing through, something you haven't felt in a long time.

A fledgling idol is being fed and is crying out for more.

I've learned that when I have any thought like that, it's time to pull back and make sure that I don't spend any more time than necessary around that person. I don't walk away, thinking, "I guess my marriage isn't meant to be. This other woman would meet my needs better." No—you have to stop at that first inkling, at that first breeze of chemistry. Right then—at that very moment—is the time to start fighting, not six months later, when the two of you are alone together in a hotel room.

Tell yourself, "This is wrong; this is sin. I made a commitment to my spouse. Christ bought me with his own blood; I have to live above my feelings and make choices that please God." Shut down those feelings, choke off your wrong thinking, by redirecting your thoughts to what the Bible says is true. Starve that idol before it grows into a monster that will take you deeper into sin than you ever thought you could go.

Tragically, the percentage of marriages going down in flames isn't any lower in the Christian community than in the rest of the world. It isn't enough simply to know that pornography is sin, that adultery is sin, that fornication is sin. You need to know something bigger than just trying to avoid those sins. You need to be aware of the idols of your heart that make you most susceptible to these sins. That's what you need to focus on, long before you're actually jumping into bed with someone other than your spouse.

Most Christians wait too long to get alarmed. They think they're okay as long as they're not getting undressed and jumping into bed, which is exactly what Satan wants them to think, so they'll keep feeding the idols that will ultimately cause them to stumble into sin. They'll say that they never saw it coming, and they're right, because they weren't focused on the right area—the heart.

I once heard Paul Tripp (while teaching from Ezekiel 14 at a conference) compare having idols in your heart to putting your hand in front of your face. They obstruct your vision; they blind you, making you far more likely to make a mistake, to stumble into iniquity.

Idols make you stupid.

It reminds me of bucks during mating season. I live in Kentucky, so I see this phenomenon played out every year. Have you ever noticed how stupid the bucks are then? And have you ever wondered why they dart right out in front of your car? Where are they going in such a hurry? What are they after? When the bucks (that's male deer for you nonhunters) are in rut (that's looking to mate), which here in Kentucky is usually mid-November, they sniff out the scent of a doe in heat, and when they find it, they take off running, throwing caution to the wind. I'm not a hunter myself, but I'm told by others in my church that a doe in heat is called a "hot" doe. I like that. But I've seen what a hot doe can do to a buck. Driving to church early one Sunday morning, I saw a buck with a big rack on his head come blazing out of someone's backyard, down the hill, and right out in front of my car. He had no flashers on, he used no turn signals, and he would have taken out my little blue Tercel if I hadn't stomped on the brakes to yield for him. So what was he after? A hot doe!

Here's an animal that spends the other 345 days of the year carefully avoiding all human contact. But during that short season, he plunges down wide-open hills, storms across four-lane highways, with absolutely no regard for cars or people, because he has only one thing on his mind: chasing down that hot doe!

Now, get this: that's a picture of us chasing down our idols. We throw caution to the wind, ignoring God's Word, ignoring loved ones who ask, "What are you doing? What are you thinking? Why would you throw it all away for this?" We don't see the barbed wire, the traffic, the open manholes, because we're focused on one thing: chasing down that idol, feeding that idol, serving that idol, protecting that idol.

But unlike the buck, who goes crazy two or three weeks out of the year, we can live stupid and chase our idols *all year long.* Some people do it for a lifetime. And then we wonder why we've got so many problems.

YOUR IDOLS RUN IN HERDS

> *". . . multitude of his idols." —Ezekiel 14:4*
>
> *"I, God, will step in and personally answer them as they come dragging along their mob of idols."*
> —The Message

Your idols keep you from seeing and avoiding sin. But how many idols are we talking about? Look at Ezekiel 14:4 again: God will answer you "according to the multitude of [your] idols." Your idols run in herds. Eugene Peterson's *The Message* paraphrases verse 4 this way: "I, God, will step in and personally answer them as they come dragging along their mob of idols." What a picture—we know that we're tired, we know that we're frustrated, and we know that life seems to have broken down. But we don't see the mob of idols that we're dragging along that are sucking the life out of us.

In Ezekiel 14:5, God says, "I have one thing I want to talk to you about." The people want to talk to him about all kinds of things. He tells Ezekiel, "Tell them I'll talk to them personally, and I want to talk to them about one thing—their idols. I want to work on their hearts." Notice who God is talking about. He says, "I want to seize the hearts of *my people*." He's not talking about the Amalekites, the Hittites, or some other "ites." He's talking about *his people*. If you are his child, you can't stray far before he comes after you. That's good news, but it can be scary news, too. He says, "I want to seize them by their hearts." The NIV says that he wants to "recapture the hearts of the people."

YOUR IDOLS CUT YOU OFF FROM GOD

> *". . . because they are all estranged from Me by their idols."* —*Ezekiel 14:5*

Do you ever feel as though God were a thousand miles away, as though your prayers were bouncing off the ceiling? Could it be that the reason for those feelings is your own idolatry?

What you need right now may not be a spiritual seminar that will jump-start your Christian life. You may not need a new study Bible or an accountability partner. What you may need is to repent of the idols in your heart that you've grown accustomed to. Your idols are crowding in between you and God. He says, "I want to seize the hearts of my people, for they are estranged from me by their idols" (Ezek. 14:5 paraphrase). Your idols cut you off from God, and he is calling you to repent. Acts 3:19 tells us, "Repent . . . , so that times of refreshing may come from the presence of the Lord."

REFLECTION AND REPENTANCE

Take a few minutes right now to think about what you have read in this chapter. What is God putting his finger on in your life? What has come to your mind as you were reading? What do you think might be causing you to stumble into iniquity? Maybe you are worn out, beaten down, and burdened. But the real issue is that you've been living with a low-grade fever of idolatry for so long that you don't know what it feels like to be healthy. The answer isn't: "Oh, God, give me more power."

The answer could be for you to repent. Repent of the idols that you've settled in with.

And when you do, you'll have a sense of God's presence again. He says, "Draw near to me and I'll draw near to you. Cleanse your hands, you sinners. Purify your hearts, you double-minded" (James 4:8 paraphrase).

Christ died to change our hearts and to save us from living on substitutes that never really satisfy. That's what the cross is for—that's why the gospel is more than words on a page. The gospel is the power of God unto salvation (Rom. 1:16), the most powerful, life-changing commodity on earth. God is saying, "Repent . . . , so that times of refreshing may come from the presence of the Lord" (Acts 3:19).

Repent right now by praying and saying:

God, today I'm laying it down. I'm letting it go. I have been gripping this thing for so long. But now I'm turning away from my idols and back to you. Lord, please refresh me. Revive me. And give me the sweet sense of your presence again in my life.

Chapter 7

Follow the Trail of Your Time, Money, and Affections

"For where your treasure is, there your heart will be also." —Matthew 6:21

We've been talking about idols, but now I want to show you how to spot them in your own life. It's a lot easier to see an idol in someone else's life, but how do you spot it in your own? What do you look for? Let's review our definition of idolatry: *An idol is anything or anyone that begins to capture our hearts, minds, and affections more than God.*

Idolatry is living on substitutes. It is exchanging the one true living God for a counterfeit. It is living out Romans 1:21–22, which says that "although they knew God, they did not glorify Him as God, nor were thankful, but became futile in their thoughts, and their foolish hearts were darkened. Professing to be wise, they became fools." Two exchanges are going on in

Romans 1: they exchanged the glory of the immortal God for images made to look like mortal men (v. 23), and they "exchanged the truth of God for the lie" (v. 25).

For our idols, we're willing to give up the glory of the one true living God. We give it up. We exchange the glory of God for something made in the likeness of man. We trade it for a child, a marriage, a job, a car. We trade in the glory of God, and we exchange the truth of God for the lie. The essence of idolatry is exchanging—and you end up with nothing but counterfeits.

Idolatry is false worship—misplaced, misdirected worship. Consider again Richard Keyes's explanation:

> At the most basic level, idols are what we make out of the evidence for God within ourselves and in the world—if we do not want to face the face of God Himself in His majesty and holiness. Rather than look to the Creator and have to deal with His lordship, we orient our lives toward the creation, where we can be more free to control and shape our lives in our desired directions. . . . However, since we were made to relate to God, but do not want to face Him, we forever inflate things in this world to religious proportions to fill the vacuum left by God's exclusion.[1]

You can't exclude God from your thinking and priorities and do well. You'll need the alcohol industry, or the pharmaceutical industry, or the sporting industry, or the entertainment industry, or some other industry to sustain you once you've abandoned God as your first love. Why? Because you need something in your life to compensate for the absence of God and the absence of a robust love for your Savior. And the alcohol, the drugs, the entertainment, the sports can never do it. They always fall short and leave you wanting more.

Whether you cross a church doorway or not, you worship before an altar. Maybe your neighbors don't go to church, but they worship—in front of the television, at the grill, or out on the lake. They're just not worshiping the God of the Bible.

Worship leader Louie Giglio pulls no punches when he says,

> Some of us attend the church on the corner, professing to worship the living God above all. Others, who rarely darken the church doors, would say worship isn't a part of their lives because they aren't "religious," but everybody has an altar. And every altar has a throne. So how do you know where and what you worship? It's easy. You simply follow the trail of your time, your affection, your energy, your money, and your allegiance. At the end of that trail you'll find a throne; and whatever, or whomever, is on that throne is what's of highest value to you. On that throne is what you worship. Sure, not too many of us walk around saying, "I worship my stuff. I worship my job. I worship pleasure. I worship her. I worship my body. I worship me." But the trail never lies. We may say we value this thing or that thing more than any other, but the volume of our actions speaks louder than our words. In the end, our worship is more about what we do than what we say.[2]

If you call yourself a Christian, and you've been around the church for a while, you've probably developed some kind of confessional theology that you would point to as what you believe. You know the right things to say: "Jesus is Lord. Live for him. Seek first the kingdom . . ." You know all that. But here's the real question: Does your functional theology—how you live your life—match your confessional theology? Does what you say you believe line up with the way you live? That's where the rubber really meets the road. Idolatry exposes the ugly disconnect between your confessional theology and your functional theology. Find your idols and you'll find out what it is you really believe.

So what does your life say? What do others see? If someone had you under surveillance—bugging your house, listening to find out what makes you mad, what brings you to tears, what makes you laugh, tracking where you invest your money and time—what would he conclude? Where would the trail lead? Would he find Jesus Christ at the end of the trail? Or would the trail lead to the ball field? Or to your computer? Would it lead to your television or your refrigerator? Would it lead to a mirror? Would there be a little shrine at the end of your trail, or maybe a fortress with a ten-foot wall?

Let me give you some more clues as you follow this trail. Whenever a legitimate desire begins to morph into an idolatrous demand, certain things will inevitably show up. And legitimate desires get Christians into trouble most of the time. For a single person, marriage is a legitimate desire. For a childless couple, children are a legitimate desire. For a person in a dead-end job, a better job is a legitimate desire. But can a legitimate desire cross the line and morph into an idolatrous demand?

You'd better believe it.

You have that desire in your hand, and you lift it to the Lord, saying, "Oh, God, you know I would love to be married. All my friends are getting married. I've been in so many weddings. I don't want to be in another wedding unless it's *my* wedding, okay? Don't give me any more silly bridesmaid's gifts—I want my own wedding. Do you understand, God?" Watch out when you start making demands of God, saying, "God, you've got until the end of this year, or we're going to have a serious talk. I'm serving You—I'm doing *my* part. Now I expect *you* to follow through with *your* part. Bring me a spouse, chop-chop."

Over time, legitimate desires turn into idolatrous demands that will bear ugly fruit in your life, and you're left wondering, "Why am I so spiritually barren? Why am I having so much trouble with the people around me? Where did the joy go?" You've moved away from the centrality of the gospel in your life. You're no longer stunned by your Savior's death and resurrection on your behalf.

Look at the following checklist and see whether anything in your life right now has changed from a simple, legitimate desire to an idolatrous demand. Whenever something in your life makes that idolatrous leap, it often shows up in one or more of the following ways:

- You'll sacrifice for it.
- You'll spend time on it.
- You'll spend money on it.
- You'll talk about it ("Out of the abundance of the heart his mouth speaks" [Luke 6:45]).
- You'll protect it/defend it.
- You'll serve it.
- You'll perfect it.
- You'll think about it.
- You'll worry about it.
- You'll get angry when someone blocks you from it or messes with it.
- You'll build your schedule around it.

Even with that list, it's still hard to judge your desires because you can say, "Wait a minute; kids are expensive. I do sacrifice for the kids; I spend money and time on the kids. Does that automatically mean they're idols?" Not necessarily. Is the amount and extent of your sacrifice inordinate? Is it keeping you from other things that God wants you to do?

Take golf, for instance. Golf costs money whether it's an idol or not. If Jonathan Edwards had played golf, even with the pure, for-the-glory-of-God attitude that I'm sure he would have played with, it still would have cost him money. So it can be a tough call to spot when something has crossed the line from legitimate pleasure to idol.

So how do you know whether golf has become an idol? I have to confess that in my own life, it's tough. I don't get to play very often, so when I'm out there on fresh-cut grass beneath a clear blue sky, and the drive goes long and straight, and the ball rolls another forty yards . . .

And by the way, there's something curiously satisfying in the sound of a well-struck ball, isn't there? Ah . . . but I digress.

More than once in my golf journey, I've been convicted to hang up the clubs. "That's it," I've said. "For me it's idolatry. I'm hanging that little bag of idols out in the garage. Goodbye, golf." Then one day I get them back down again, thinking, "I'm okay, really—I'm over the golf-idol thing now; I can do this." Then after playing some more, I realize that I'm not okay—I make a bad shot, and it makes me so stinking mad. But how do I really know that golf has crossed the line and become an idol for me?

Okay, here's how I know. Golf goes bad for Brad when I find myself thinking about it all the time. It's when I fall asleep thinking through all eighteen holes of the last round I played, revisiting each shot. Or it's when I begin to anticipate the next time I'm going to play, days or even weeks before. I can't wait—I've got my shoes out; I've got the socks I'm going to wear with them. I'm buffing balls; I'm going through all the zippers in my bag, making sure I've got enough tees, power bars, and waters. Basically, it's too big a deal.

And I think golf is becoming an idol when I'm driving to work on one of those gorgeous days when the flowers seem brighter than usual, and the sky is so blue, and my mind starts racing: "How can I play golf today?" I know I have meetings, I know there are shattered lives that need to meet with me, but I don't care—

I just want to play golf.

All I care about is figuring out how I can play golf today. Maybe I can rearrange or cancel my appointments. Oh, wait—I'll play with a lost guy, so it will really be evangelism. Or I'll take my son with me, so it will be a father-son thing, and the wife will love that, and—bonus—it will get the boy out of the house, too. It's a win-win.

Do you see what's happening? I'm consumed and driven by golf. But only the gospel and my Savior should consume my thoughts like that. Obsession with anything or anyone else is high treason in light of what God has done for me in Christ.

You know you've crossed the line when you begin to plot and scheme and connive. Or when it rains on the day you were supposed to play golf, and you find yourself ripping mad about it. You don't want to do anything else; you're inconsolable. You were going to golf today, and now it's raining. Game over.

This doesn't apply just to golf, of course; you can take my thoughts and attitudes about golf and apply them to working on your car, to your job, shopping, exercising, going on a date, or an infinite number of other things. So when does it become idolatry for you? Be honest, and then follow the trail of your time, money, and affections. That trail doesn't lie, and it always leads you to an altar.

CHAPTER 8

LOOK FOR CHAOS!

"For where envy and self-seeking exist, confusion and every evil thing are there." —James 3:16

Idols bring chaos like rats bring disease. Chaos and confusion. You have chaos in your life, particularly in your relationships, and you don't know why. Chaos and confusion almost always have idolatry lurking behind them. Why? Because idolatry of the heart creates war. James 4:1 asks, "Where do wars and fights come from among you?" James isn't talking about a world war; he's not talking about a civil war. He's talking about war between individuals—such as between husband and wife, parent and child, neighbor and neighbor, boss and employee.

"Where do wars and fights come from among you? Do they not come from your desires . . . ?" You want something, but your wife is getting in the way of it, so you've got a problem. You want something, and your kids are getting in the way of it. And suddenly you have war.

IDOLATRY CREATES CONFUSION WITH EVERYONE AROUND YOU

Your idols create confusion with the people around you because you're so quick to either erupt with anger or pull back with manipulation and pouting, and they can't figure out what they did to cause it. Maybe they *did* do something to set you off, but they don't see the full picture. They can't see the idols in your heart, idols that so easily drive your fear and discontentment into eruptions of anger or tears. You're afraid that your idolatrous desires aren't going to be fulfilled, so you respond the way you do because your idols are the most important things to you. But because you don't wear a sign around your neck that says, "Beware—Here are my top five idols—Stay back fifty feet," those around you don't know what's going on.

Idolatry causes confusion.

UNCHECKED IDOLS LEAD TO UGLY EXPLOSIONS

One Christmas, the idols of my heart led to a public outburst in an Olan Mills Photography waiting room in Knoxville, Tennessee. You have to wonder: what would lead a meek, godly, humble, wonderful husband like me to blow up at such a lovely creature as my wife? There was no profanity, nor did it come to blows, but what a scene I made! I was standing in the waiting room with my mom, dad, twin brother, younger brother, aunts, uncles, cousins—along with many other people I don't even know, but people who no doubt still talk about it to this day! Yes, it was that ugly.

So what set me off? What triggered such an outburst? Check this out: my wife slipped over to me and asked, "Honey, on the way back to your parents' house, could we . . ." Now, let me insert a little aside here. You've got to understand—I *really* didn't want to be there. This was back when I got only five days' vacation, and one of those days—every Christmas when we would visit my parents—had to be spent dressing the whole family up and going to Olan Mills so that my mom could get the free 8×10. Nobody else got anything because we didn't buy the rest of the package. So it's a half day spent on this picture thing, every Christmas—dressing up, getting the kids ready, dragging ourselves over there. It doesn't excuse my sin, but believe me when I say that I really didn't want to be there.

But there was much more to it than that.

What was the question that lit my fuse? Vicki asked, "On the way back to your parents' house, could we stop and get diapers?" Hmmm. So I erupted, and I didn't care who saw it. My voice escalated as I told her, "You should have thought of that before now, and you should have already gotten the diapers! *That's your job . . . blah, blah, blah, blah!*" Confusion and chaos in the Olan Mills waiting room, and the festive Christmas sweater I was wearing couldn't mask what I was spewing all over Vicki and everyone else in the room.

That doesn't make sense, does it? What set me off like that? What's the big deal with stopping for diapers? Did I have a chemical imbalance? Was I bipolar? No. You see, I didn't know it at the time, but some idols had taken root in my heart, idols that got more and more entrenched as my thinking continued down the same old sinful path—so I went *kaboom!*

Here's the deal. I was in seminary full time, while living in a trailer so tiny that if I bumped into a wall, pieces would fall off. I was taking Hebrew and Greek at the same time, and to top it off, the senior pastor had been asked to resign, so the church leaders asked me to fulfill his responsibilities—preach, visit the hospitals, along with youth and music—just long enough for us to find somebody else.

And of course it took eighteen months to find that somebody else.

In the meantime, I was carrying a full load of classes, serving as youth and worship leader, helping with preaching and pastoral duties, and dealing with everything involved in running a home and family. So on top of everything going on at church and school, I was at home changing the oil in the '72 Buick Skylark that ran only half the time and balancing the checkbook—unaware that an idol was creeping into my heart. I had unconsciously begun to tell myself, "No one else should put any more demands on me. Period. I can't do another thing—I shouldn't *have* to do another thing. Everyone should see all that I'm doing, especially those closest to me. They should only serve me, not make any more demands of me."

Do you see where all this was headed? I had never voiced this. I had never taken Vicki out to a candlelit dinner and said, "Honey, I need you to understand the point that I've reached now. Here's where we are. You can't make any more demands of me." We don't notify each other of these things; we don't give people a heads-up. In my own heart, it was the idol of "I deserve a break; no one should demand anything else of me—especially those closest to me! Just feel bad for me. Tell me how hard I have it. Ask if there's anything you can do to help me."

And so I erupted when my wife added one more thing.

An outburst of anger or extreme emotion is always an opportunity; it's an alarm bell for you to take notice and to assess what's going on in your heart. Trace the lava of your anger back to your heart and ask, "Are things okay in my heart? What is in there that I'm not aware of? Something's going on, because most of the time I express these strong emotions when I'm protecting or losing something I've decided that I absolutely have to have."

Happily, I can't remember the last time I erupted in anger toward my wife like that, but where do you think I'm now most prone to erupt? Hint: I'm the father of five children (three of them teenagers). When there's a fight or a bad attitude, when people are failing to fulfill their responsibilities, when we just don't feel like that happy, wonderful, humming-along family, it ticks me off. It makes me mad because I'm telling myself, "I'm so sick of them getting into fights; why can't they just get along? I shouldn't have to deal with this; they have such a bad attitude, and this isn't the way I taught them to behave." So then godly Pastor Dad steps in and brings peace, by erupting and spewing biblical rebukes on everyone who needs it and some who don't. I end up rebuking everyone in the van, the house, the yard—you name it. And by the time I'm done, the kids' fight is over, and they're all looking at me like I have two heads, thinking, "Whoa, look at him go. Don't you hate it when he does this?" Then a deathly silence settles over the van or the house or wherever this unhappy scene takes place.

So what's going on there?

It's the idol of "I shouldn't have to repeat myself. I shouldn't have to retrain, remind, or tell you again. I shouldn't have to unravel problems. Just do what you're supposed to do—what I've trained you to do—every time, all the time, without exception. I've been telling you this since you were a fetus in the womb. Hello, put your shoes away, put the keys on the hook. I shouldn't have to keep telling you this, and the fact that I have to stop what I'm doing right now and say it again really makes me mad."

And then God says to me, "Hello, am I still having to tell you things that I've been saying to you since you first sucked air into your lungs?"

IDOLATRY LURKS BEHIND THE CONFUSION AND CHAOS IN OUR RELATIONSHIPS

So what am I thinking when I expect these things of my kids? What am I saying myself? Can you see the idolatry that's lurking behind these outbursts? Now, don't get me wrong—the kids need to change and grow; they need to put the shoes in the basket and the keys on the hook. But more importantly, there is an idol in my heart that needs to die.

It could be that God has a bigger agenda at work, one that includes making sure that the shoes don't get in the basket and the keys don't get on the hook—until that idol in my heart dies.

My kids could say to me, "Father, it's your own idolatry that hinders us. We could be more obedient if you were more repentant. God's not allowing us to do these things properly and consistently, Father." Now, that would really tick me off, but there would probably be a grain of truth in it. So often, God is probably looking down, thinking, "I don't care whether the shoes are at the front door or in the basket; your ugly heart is a bigger concern to me right now."

So first, *follow the trail of your time, money, and affections*. Second, *look for chaos*. Third, *ask yourself some heart-diagnostic questions*.

ASK YOURSELF SOME HARD QUESTIONS

The three questions that we previously encountered in chapter 2 can help you detect an idol in your heart:

1. Am I willing to sin to get it?
2. Am I willing to sin if I think I'm going to lose it?
3. Do I run to it for refuge instead of to God?

Are You Willing to Sin to Get It?

Are you willing to work seventy or eighty hours a week to be the flavor of the month and win the boss's attention—even if your family is suffering, your spiritual life is withering, and you've lost all sight of ministry at work?

Are You Willing to Sin if You Think You're Going to Lose It?

For example, good health is a good thing, and it's something that we usually start off with. But later in life we start to lose it. Are you willing to spend inordinate amounts of time at the gym and money that you don't have on supplements? Or do you see an ad and think, "If I use *this*, my skin will look younger; I won't have those brown spots anymore"? Or maybe you have an illness or disease. How much should you work at alleviating it? Don't get me wrong. It's not a sin to seek out doctors and treatment. But could you cross a line to a place where you begin to live only to find a cure?

Do You Run to It for Refuge instead of to God?

In December 2002, I began to lose hearing in my right ear, and it has now spread to the left ear as well. I've gone to doctors, specialists, and audiologists. Finally, a specialist in Cincinnati diagnosed my condition as *patulous Eustachian tube*, which really has no cure. So I did what most other people today would do—I turned the Internet upside down looking for treatments. But the breakthrough in my life was not some elixir or some magic cure from the Internet. It was a prayer I wrote one morning in my prayer journal. I prayed, "God, I give you my hearing. If you have a better plan, if there's a way I can bring you more glory by not hearing—then you decide. I trust you." Oh, I've cried.

I've prayed. I've fasted. And I've still battled fear and depression over the whole situation. But that one prayer ushered me into a place of peace that couldn't be found on the Internet.

Your struggle may not be with your hearing, but you might be gripping something else so tightly that you need to turn it over to God and say, "God, you decide." Ask yourself: "Am I willing to sin to get it? Am I willing to sin if I think I'm going to lose it? And do I run to it as a refuge?"

KEEP LOOKING TO THE CROSS!

So what's the answer to our idolatry? The cross. Christ died on the cross to set us free from living on substitutes, to set us free from cramped hearts that are full of idols. So celebrate what Christ did for us! And remember, as Ed Welch said, "The path of change goes through the heart and continues on to the gospel, where God most fully reveals to us his Son Jesus Christ in the death and resurrection of Christ."[1] We want to continue on to the gospel. The gospel is our only hope if we're to escape wasting our life in pursuit of counterfeits. Don't just say "no" to idols; say "yes" to all that Christ is for you in the gospel. Preach the gospel to yourself every day. Turn it over in your mind. Hold it up to the light of God's glory, and like a gem let it refract shafts of powerful, life-giving color into your dark heart that's crowded with idols.

Chapter 9

DON'T DARE FOLLOW YOUR HEART

At the heart of idolatry is a lack of trusting God. Here's the bottom line: Are you going to worship God, follow God, and trust God? Or are you going to cling to your idols and build your world around them? We go other places besides God, cling to other things and people and circumstances for our security. It isn't just unbelievers who don't trust God—often, believers don't really trust him, either.

So easily and so quickly our trust drifts. It has to be continually renewed and put back in the right spot. Trust drifts. And it never drifts toward God; it's always away from him and toward our idols. And your failure to trust God doesn't just affect your relationship with God; it affects how you respond to your wife and kids, how you respond to that health problem, and how you respond to that financial setback.

What you want, what you think, and what you say to yourself *in your heart* makes the difference. Remember that *an idol is anything or anyone that begins to capture our hearts, minds, and affections more than God.*

SO WHAT ARE WE REALLY TALKING ABOUT WHEN WE TALK ABOUT THE HEART?

"For as he thinks in his heart, so is he."—Proverbs 23:7

If we're going to get our hands around this desire that leads to sin, then we need to trace it back to the heart. But as I keep using the word *heart*, you may need to flush from your mind every prior definition you have of what *heart* means. In our culture—on television, in the movies, in music and popular writing—the heart is presented as a safe haven, a place you can trust.

Think about it. In almost every Hallmark made-for-television movie, in the pivotal scene, the lead character is going to be asked—whether in the living room or out on the farm leaning against a split-rail fence—"What is your heart saying to you?" A daughter is trying to decide whether to go with this boy or not, or whether to take that great job in New York, leaving behind all that she's known—what does her mother or her best friend tell her?

"Listen to your heart."

Ah! But that's wrong, absolutely wrong. Hollywood gets it exactly wrong and gives us the worst possible advice—but it sounds so right, doesn't it? It appeals to our flesh. It appeals to our human reasoning. And Hollywood isn't the only one pushing this trust-your-heart propaganda. Turn on the radio and you'll get a steady dose of the same nonsense. So much of our music is wrapped around this same theme.

But the Bible teaches that your heart will land you in a mess of sin and far away from God. Don't listen to it. Listen to God's Word—because, as Jeremiah reminds us, "the heart is . . . desperately wicked" (Jer. 17:9).

GUIDE IT, GUARD IT, BUT PLEASE DON'T FOLLOW IT

"He who trusts in his own heart is a fool, but whoever walks wisely will be delivered." —Proverbs 28:26

The world keeps pointing us back to the heart, and so does the Bible. But here's the difference: the Bible points us back to the heart with a very different mission from what the world has in mind. The Bible tells us to direct our heart toward God's ways. Go to your heart to inspect it and direct it, but don't dare follow it. Go there to rein it in. Don't go there listening; go there talking and speaking truth from God's Word.

Jeremiah 17:9 observes, "The heart is deceitful above all things, and desperately wicked; who can know it?" If that's the condition of your heart, then what should you do with it? Follow it? Listen to it? I don't think so. The book of Proverbs lists three things that we're supposed to do with our heart: *Guide it, guard it, but do not follow it.*

Look at Proverbs 23:19: "Hear, my son, and be wise; and guide your heart in the way." *Guide* it. The world would have you believe that the heart is this thing that you have no control over. But God says to guide it.

Proverbs 4:23 warns, "Guard your heart above all else, for it determines the course of your life" (NLT). As your heart goes, so you go. So *guard* it, take charge of it, direct it. Find out what God's Word says—and whether you feel like it or not, whether it seems right to you or not, take your heart, and *you* move *it* in the direction that God's Word says. Say, "Heart, listen up. We're going God's way. I'm not listening to you anymore; I'm not following you anymore. I'm directing you. And if I have to, I'll drag you kicking and screaming in the direction of God's Word."

Proverbs 28:26 asserts, "He who trusts in his own heart is a . . ." made-for-television movie star? No—"He who trusts in his own heart is a *fool*, but whoever walks wisely will be delivered." Guide it, guard it, and do not trust or follow it. See, your heart is not your best friend. Jesus Christ, speaking through his Word, is your best friend.

In fact, the Bible tells you to maintain a healthy suspicion toward your heart, while maintaining a powerful respect and appreciation for God's Word, a steadfast submission to God's Word. Ask yourself, "What should I do in this situation? How should I handle this? What does God's Word say?" Don't listen to your heart. Your heart will tell you, "Run away! This is no fun. This is hard." Or else: "Go for it. This is what you want. This will make you happy." That's where we are in our culture today. Everybody is following his own heart and making a big, fat mess. Listening to your heart will lead you from one relationship to the next, and one job to the next, and one disaster to the next, with no end in sight. Guide your heart, guard it, but don't dare follow it.

YOUR HEART IS THE PROCESSING CENTER

But why is the heart such a mess, and so given to idols? I want to give you two reasons why your heart is so susceptible to idols. We'll cover one reason in this chapter, and the other in chapter 10. The first reason you're so susceptible to idols is that *your heart is the processing and sorting center for everything you do and everything you'll become.* Look at the "How Do We Process Life?" diagram on page 144, and let me explain how this works.

Stimuli: You Can't Keep Life from Happening around You

Let's start with stimuli, and we'll work our way around the circle. Stuff happens. You can't keep life from happening around you, and God doesn't call us to live in a bubble or a Christian convent. Like it or not, life happens around you, nonstop. People hurt you, best friends desert you, health fails you, finances take wings and fly away, jobs evaporate. Stuff happens, and it is relentless.

Thinking: Your Heart Never Stops Trying to Make Sense of It All

So what do you do? The next step on the circle is thinking—your heart never stops thinking, never stops trying to make sense of life as it happens. Because we're created in the image of God, we are interpreters. We're not dogs or peacocks or aardvarks. Stuff happens, and animals just roll over and scratch and yawn. They just eat, poop, sleep, breed. But human beings are created in the image of God, so we are not satisfied with just eating, sleeping, and reproducing. We want to know why things happen the way they do, why we're here, and what this thing called *life* is all about. Our hearts never stop trying to make sense of it all.

That's why some of the things children say are so hilarious. Often, the things they say are funny because they've drawn a wrong conclusion, which proves that their little brains have been processing what's going on around them and trying to make sense of it. After my grandfather died, my grandmother moved in with my parents. Shortly afterward, when my oldest daughter, Lauren, was three years old, we were there visiting for the holidays. We were all gathered around the table sharing a big meal, with lots of conversation going, and Lauren sat quietly, taking it all in. Though we weren't talking to her directly, she was picking up on the things being discussed. At some point we talked with Grandma about how sad it was without Grandpa there. At another point, it came up that she didn't have a car, but no one made a big deal of it, since she'd never had one.

Grandpa had always done all the driving. We talked about the peace and joy of knowing that Grandpa was in heaven. Later, as I was kissing Lauren goodnight and tucking her into bed, she said, "We need to pray for Grandma, because Grandpa died and took the car to heaven with him."

Her little mind and heart were trying to connect the dots and make sense out of everything she'd heard—she put the pieces together in a way that made sense to a three-year-old. We're no different. We're constantly trying to put the pieces together. We're not satisfied with just dumping the puzzle out on the table and leaving it there—we want to make sense of it. We want to see how it all fits together.

The problem is, like my daughter, we don't always come to the right conclusions. Notice in the diagram that I drew a heart around *thinking*. That's what the Bible teaches. When the Bible talks about the *heart*, it's talking about thinking—desire, will, motives—who you really are, what you want, and what you say to yourself.

Whether we're conscious of it or not, we're constantly talking to ourselves, assessing, evaluating, and thinking at an incredible rate throughout the day. You're telling yourself, "This isn't fair. This makes no sense. Where's God right now?" Or: "I deserve better than this. This shouldn't be happening." Or: "I can't handle this." We're constantly talking to ourselves. And that's what the Bible means when it speaks of the heart.

Our thoughts are the control center that the Bible speaks about, and Scripture uses the words *heart* and *mind* interchangeably. It's the same thing in the Old Testament. When the Bible speaks of our emotions, it places the emotions in the bowels, the intestines, the kidneys—digestive organs. In our culture, we talk about the heart on Valentine's Day. They would have talked about their kidneys. A romantic Israelite would have sent his sweetheart a Valentine's Day card that said, "Baby, you put a quiver in my liver and make me want to shiver." They placed the emotions in the digestive organs because that's where we *feel* stuff. We're just not used to thinking about emotions in our guts. We don't say, "Whoa, you make my large intestine move!" We just don't think or talk that way. But if you think about it, placing the seat of emotions in the gut is much more accurate than in the heart. Where do you feel it when you're nervous about a test you're about to take, or a race you're about to run, or a meeting you're about to have? In your gut—in the pit of your stomach.

But the Bible places thinking in the heart. Proverbs 23:7 observes, "For as he [a man or woman] thinks in his heart, so is he." We already looked at Proverbs 4:23, which says, "Guard your heart above all else, for it determines the course of your life" (NLT). It's what you think, what you desire. Have you ever noticed how often the Bible talks about speaking to yourself in your heart? Your heart is where you do your thinking, processing, assessing. Psalm 15:1–2 says:

> LORD, who may abide in Your tabernacle?
> Who may dwell in Your holy hill?
>
> He who walks uprightly,
>   And works righteousness,
>   And speaks the truth in his heart.

According to Obadiah 3:

> The pride of your heart has deceived you,
>
> . . . .
>
> [you] who say in your heart,
> "Who will bring me down to the ground?"

The thoughts that we say to ourselves we say in our hearts. The heart is where we do our thinking, talking, sorting, and interpreting of everything that life is throwing at us. We do what we do because we want what we want, and we want what we want because we think what we think. Our actions stem from what we're feeding our hearts. So the heart is our control center.

And that means that when we sin, it's never random. It might seem random when you can't see the heart, but there is no random sin. There are no random acts of violence. There are no random outbursts of anger, no random flights of fear, no random flood of tears. It's not random. You were already thinking something in your heart long before you felt something and acted on it.

Emotions: Your Feelings Feed Off Your Thinking

You can't stop things from happening all around you, and your heart never stops trying to make sense out of it, and that inevitably leads to the third step—your feelings feed off your thinking. Based on what you've been thinking, you start experiencing fear, anxiety, worry, depression, envy, or anger. Thinking is the fuel that feeds emotions. These two things aren't disconnected; our feelings flow out of our thinking.

I know there are instances when people are depressed and have a black-cloud-hanging-over-their-life kind of feeling as the result of something organic. That's not what I have in mind here. And there are instances, which the Bible speaks of in Psalms 77 and 88, of what the Puritans called the "dark night of the soul," in which godly people go through a long, horrible sense of darkness. These are people who love God and cling to his Word, saying, "Search me and know my heart. Try me. See if there's been any wicked way" (Ps. 139:23–24 paraphrase). God is in control, and for whatever reason, he is allowing them to go through a dark time. I have seen very godly and mature people go through this. So don't jump up from reading this book and blast someone you know who is taking a psychotropic drug, saying, "Grow up! Get big in Christ. Read his Word and stop taking that stuff."

I'm speaking in general, because our culture in general turns to medication immediately as its first recourse, instead of saying, "Wait a minute . . . what else is going on inside me?" Many people could be greatly helped by asking questions of the heart, because the danger of taking the pill immediately is that they might feel better immediately, and say, "I'm okay now. I don't need counseling or biblical introspection to work this out." That's what we want to avoid, because in many cases they haven't gotten to the heart of the problem.

In his book *The Reign of Grace*, Scotty Smith puts it this way:

> Paying careful attention to emotions that grow to near neurotic proportions is one of the most effective ways to identify specific idols. Whether manifested as spontaneous outbursts or chronic life patterns, these exaggerated emotions can provide an unobstructed view into the cathedral of our idol worship. The main questions to ask ourselves in light of such intense feelings are, "What do I think I have to have in life beyond Jesus and what he chooses to give me? Has something or someone become too important to me . . . ?" When anger gets out of control, ask yourself, "What am I being blocked from having that I believe is a necessity but really isn't? Marriage, children, success, a Ph.D., a record deal?" If fear threatens to overwhelm you, ask, "What is being threatened that I think is essential but really isn't? My 401K, my life, my physical looks, my reputation?" If despondency consumes you, consider: "What have I lost that I believe is critical to have but really isn't? A starting position on the football team, my spouse's approval,

> my parents, the ability to drive a golf ball three hundred yards, my wrinkleless face?"[1]

Emotions give us an occasion to trace back behind them to find out what's going on in the heart. What would produce that level of emotion? Emotions are heart indicators to alert us that there's a problem. Think of emotions as your spiritual sense of smell; how often have you said, "Do you smell that? Is something burning?" Our sense of smell alerts us that there's a problem. And in the same way, our emotions alert us that there is a problem—in our heart.

I love tuna. I used to eat tuna all the time, straight-up tuna out of the can—no mayo, no relish, just tuna. I open a can, drain the juice in the sink, and eat it. My wife hates tuna, even the smell of it. So after I've drained my tuna, she wants the sink rinsed and scoured. She doesn't even want the can in the kitchen garbage. I have to take it far, far away. So one day, my wife called me at church and said, "Honey, did you drop an empty tuna can in the kitchen garbage, or spill some tuna juice? We're dying here—I mean, it just reeks, like dead fish or something rotten."

And since we were homeschooling at the time, I was told the kids couldn't even do school. They couldn't think for the stink.

I said, "No, I haven't had tuna, and I certainly didn't spill any."

So she cleaned out the freezer, but still didn't find the source of the odor. She pulled out the refrigerator to see whether something had rolled under there, but found nothing.

We couldn't figure it out.

I had recently put out poison for carpenter ants, and I wondered whether they had all marched into the house and croaked inside the walls, but then I thought, "Dead ants don't stink." So I thought maybe a chipmunk or a squirrel had eaten some of the poison, crawled into our house, and died—but the mystery was that the smell would come and go; it would be there, and then it wouldn't be there. I'd come home around five o'clock and say, "I don't smell anything." But my family would claim that it had been there earlier.

Then one day the smell started while I was home, and someone screamed, "It's here, it's here! Stand here in the kitchen. You smell it?" And I did. But I couldn't figure out what it was.

Someone told us that it was probably mold in the attic, so I put on my gear and prepared to do what I think is the hardest job in the world—crawl through the attic. You can't walk in an attic like ours; you just crawl across the joists, trying not to put your foot through the ceiling. I was burning up, crawling through blown insulation with a broom handle, a little grocery sack, and a flashlight, so that if I found something dead, I could bag it. But there was nothing—no mold, no dead animal.

And then it happened. A few days later I was standing on a step stool to change a bulb in the kitchen ceiling light, and the globe was so hot, you could fry an egg on it. So I took the globe off and started to unscrew the burned-out bulb, but it was so hot, I couldn't touch it. Then I took a good look at the light. What used to be white was now a smoky, yellowish brown. And there, standing on the step stool, I realized that we'd put seventy-watt bulbs in a fixture that called for forty-watt bulbs. The little sticker said forty-watt maximum, but I took that as a suggestion. I like it bright. So a few weeks earlier, I had switched the lower wattage bulbs to seventy-watt bulbs, and we'd all stood around and raved about how much better it was. You could land airplanes in our kitchen, it was so bright.

But danger and trouble had been smoldering. The plastic molding around the base of the three bulbs was actually melting. And the awful smell that we couldn't trace for so long was the smell of burning plastic and electrical parts. We had been living at risk, and it was my fault. We had been blaming the smell of burning plastic and electrical parts on ants and mold and dead rodents, when *I* was the cause of it. I had done it. I was the source of the problem.

That's the same way it is with us in our hearts. Emotions signal us that something is wrong, and we start looking everywhere else, blaming other people, blaming our circumstances—but it's us. The trouble is, when we're serving our idols, they do please us to some degree, and so life seems brighter. But we don't recognize that the smell of death—the burning that surrounds our life—is an indication that something's wrong. There's trouble; we just don't realize it's our idols. Our idols are the root of the problem.

Actions: They're Rarely Ever Bizarre

You can't stop life from happening all around you. Your heart continually tries to make sense of it; your feelings feed off your thinking, and then you act. This means that your actions are rarely ever bizarre. The world is quick to give some bizarre explanation—schizophrenia, bipolar disorder, multiple personality disorder. But your actions are rarely ever bizarre. If you knew what was going on in your heart and how you have been interpreting life, it would make total sense to you why you did what you did. Once again, your actions are rarely ever bizarre. Actions flow directly out of what you've been thinking and feeling.

Character: Shaped by the Patterns of Your Heart

If you continue to think, emote, and act (T.E.A.) in the same direction, your character will eventually be shaped by the dominant patterns of your heart.

Here's what I mean. All of us have gotten angry at some point in our lives. But you probably know someone that you'd describe as "an angry man" or "an angry woman." This person has been angry so much and going that same route for so long that it becomes what he thinks, how he feels, and then how he acts. So when a circumstance comes up, one little trigger is all it takes to send him down the path of thinking, feeling, and acting—then, *boom!* That pattern of angry behavior is there, and he says, "It's just who I am. I can't help it."

And it feels that way to him because it's so immediate; it has become rooted in his very nature. It has become a habit that's rooted in his character. But for the Christian, that's never, ever true. The place to attack and begin work is back at the beginning. Ask yourself how you have been processing life. How have you been interpreting things? What are you wanting? What are you thinking? What are you demanding? What are you worshiping? What are you clinging to other than God?

Your anger is not who you are. But it's what you become as you beat a well-worn path in the same direction—from your heart out into your actions and attitudes—to the point that it characterizes you.

If anything other than God and his precious gospel becomes your vision, if anything else begins to rule the landscape of your heart, you will find yourself in trouble. You will be frustrated. You will be fearful. And you'll wonder, "Why doesn't God help me to get what I need? I'm anxious; I don't feel secure. I need God to provide this." But he'll block you and he'll frustrate you if something other than God is your vision, if something other than God has taken preeminence in your heart. That's the place to look. That's the place to start. Ask God to help you.

Lord, I pray that you would do heart surgery on me, enable me to see my heart as you see it. God, I pray that you would expose the idols there. Lord, I don't want to go there to listen to my heart. I don't want to go there to follow, submit to, or trust my heart. God, show me my heart so that I can direct it in your ways, so that I can guide it, guard it, but certainly not trust in it. I want to trust in you. Forgive me for trusting in other things and turning from you. Bring me back, God. I pray in Jesus' name. Amen.

"HOW DO WE PROCESS LIFE?"

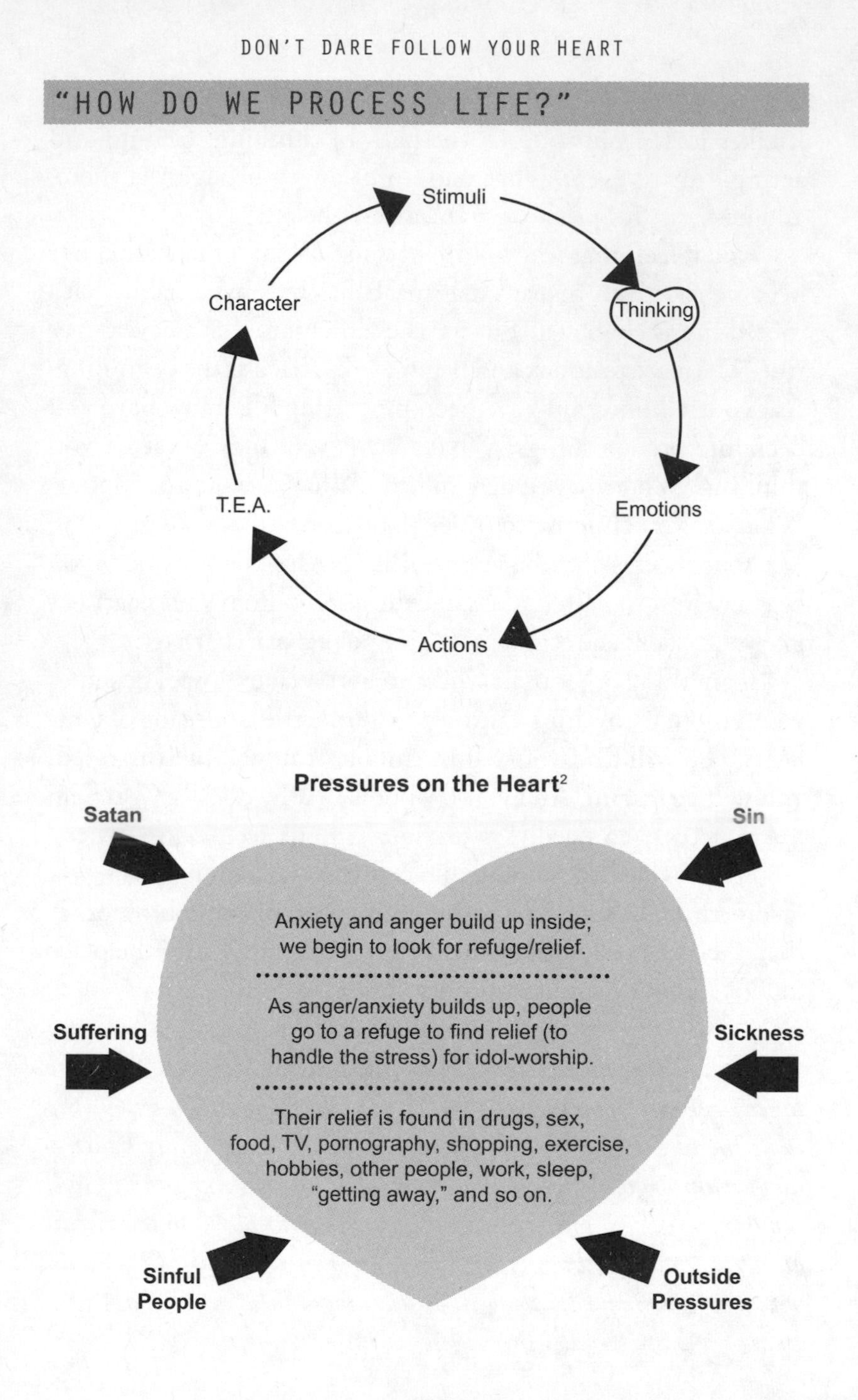

AN EXAMPLE OF WHERE FOLLOWING YOUR HEART WILL GET YOU

Panic Attack or Panic Payback?

Let me give you an example of how our thinking can feed and fuel our emotions to the point of being sinfully ruled by them. Our world calls any sudden, debilitating, paralyzing fear a *panic attack*. We didn't hear that term when I was a little boy—you were just plain-old "scared to death." Now we have a new label that makes it sound like something that no one has ever dealt with before, and we think, "Well, God's Word doesn't say anything about panic attacks." That's part of the problem with relabeling everything. We say, "Okay, it's a panic attack," as if some bizarre thing just jumped on you out of the blue and you had nothing to do with it.

I'll give you a better term than *panic attack*—*panic payback*, or *panic paycheck*: the culmination of all you've been thinking and wanting and desiring and fretting over in your heart, long before—*bam!*—panic hits you. I'm not saying that it doesn't *feel* like an attack. I know it does, because it comes on so suddenly, and with such surprising force, because we're not conscious of what we've been thinking. And maybe what you've been thinking—what you've been telling yourself, the way you've been processing life, the way you've been interpreting everything that has happened to you—has been building up since you were a child. And now, in response to a painful divorce or some other rejection, everything you've been thinking since you were a child has suddenly overloaded your system. The way you've been processing life has caught up with you, and has built up to the point that your emotions have had enough—and *boom!* You've got a full-blown panic attack on your hands.

Have Enough Compassion to Call It Sinful Fear

The most compassionate thing we can do is to cut through the confusion and psychobabble, and bring it back to what's really going on. It's your thinking that has fed your emotions long enough to cause them to erupt in fear. And I'm not making light of it. I'm not saying, "It's just good old-fashioned fear. Get on your knees and repent. Stop being afraid." But what I am saying is that the most loving thing we can do for someone going through this is to help the person to understand that it's not some bizarre thing. We must call it what the Bible calls it, and find hope in doing so. When you call it what the Bible calls it, you can trace it back to the heart and begin to unravel that gnarly ball of thread. You may not understand all that has led to this point, but start pulling the pieces apart and say, "Let's figure out what you have been saying to yourself, what you've been wanting, how you've been processing life." And you'll almost always find that the interpretation and the process have left God out of the picture, or so far out in the margin that he's not a real player.

Christians can be as guilty as anyone else of processing life without regard to God and his Word. We go to church, we sing the songs, we testify of God's sovereignty, his goodness, his mercy, his power. Yet we go out on Monday morning and process life without bringing any of those great truths to bear on our personal situation. It's as though worship were a separate segment of life that's only for Sunday, a segment that rarely intersects with the deep hurt we're facing right now in our life. That's the battle: taking the truth of who God is, and what his Word says, and applying it right in that moment of struggle—right then, right there.

See God in the Problem

You've got to see God in the problem. So don't call it a panic attack, and don't say that your emotions aren't working right.

You just proved that they work the way God designed them to work, and now they are cashing in on all the wrong thinking that you've invested in a certain account for so long. If you think something long enough, and repeat it to yourself loudly enough and often enough, your emotions will rise up, knock you to the mat, and leave the fat man of fear sitting on your chest. You gasp, "I can't breathe. What's going on? Get him off," but you're the one who fed that fear—you're the one who made him so fat. You've got a sumo-sized fear squeezing the life out of you now, but it started with your own thinking.

And so now you're the one who has to put him on a diet.

The way to slim him down and roll him off your chest is to cut off his food supply—your wrong thinking.

Remember—your thinking feeds your emotions.

Chapter 10

Recognize Where Your Heart Is Most Vulnerable

Why do you sin the way you sin? Why do you get hung up where you get hung up? And why is it so hard to stop, even when God by his Holy Spirit convicts you? And however much effort you put forth, why do you find yourself going back to the same sin again and again?

Remember: *An idol is anything or anyone that begins to capture our hearts, minds, and affections more than God.* It's living on substitutes. It's exchanging the glory of the one true living God—his majesty, his power, his goodness, his promises, and all that he does in our lives—for something else, for a boyfriend, a girlfriend, a spouse, a job, athletic achievement, financial stability, health, or just an idea. And idolatry shows up in a million different places in our lives. As John Calvin said, "The heart is a factory of idols."[1]

In the previous chapter, we saw that the first reason your heart is so susceptible to idols is that your heart is the processing and sorting center for everything you do and everything you become. Remember the circle we looked at about how we process life? Look at it again. That is the circle of life, and it is repeated over and over throughout a person's lifetime. Most people are stuck somewhere in that circle. They want to change, but they don't know where to begin. They don't like the fruits or the harvest that comes from the way they're living, but they don't know how to go about effecting lasting change that's more than just rearranging stuff on the surface.

But God gives us the same answer every time: start with the heart. Now, obviously, behavior that is injurious to others or to oneself, behavior that is illegal and dangerous, must be stopped immediately. But once you've stopped the behavior, you had better get to the heart or it will be back, bigger and uglier than ever!

YOUR HEART IS THE COMPASS THAT POINTS TO WHERE YOU RUN UNDER PRESSURE

> *"No temptation has overtaken you except such as is common to man; but God is faithful, who will not allow you to be tempted beyond what you are able, but with the temptation will also make the way of escape, that you may be able to bear it. Therefore, my beloved, flee from idolatry."*
> *—1 Corinthians 10:13–14*

Now, with that foundation, I want to give you a second reason that our hearts are so susceptible to idols: *your heart is the compass that points to where you run under pressure.* It exposes something about us. The needle points in a certain direction under pressure.

In 1 Corinthians 10, the apostle Paul, inspired by the Holy Spirit, makes a connection between temptations and idols. He connects the dots. First Corinthians 10:13 teaches, "No temptation has overtaken you except such as is common to man; but

God is faithful, who will not allow you to be tempted beyond what you are able, but with the temptation will also make the way of escape, that you may be able to bear it." But notice verse 14: "Therefore, my beloved, flee from idolatry."

What is Paul doing here? Why is he jumping from temptations to idols? Because Paul understands something inspired by the Holy Spirit—he knows that when the pressure is on, when we are being tempted, we look for an outlet, a relief, a place of refuge. So if we're not on guard, our first thought and our first inclination is to run to something earthly—we run to our spouse and demand that our needs be met there; we turn to our job and throw ourselves into it and work more; we turn to some substance or pill or alcohol; we turn to the television or the Internet and try to lose ourselves there—we turn to earthly things instead of God when we're under pressure, because they are easier and quicker.

And they are visible.

You can see your spouse, so it's easy to cling to her and demand more out of that relationship. It's easy to turn to your job—you go there every day anyway—and so you pour yourself more heavily into it. And God knows, therein lies the great danger: when the pressure's on, if we're not careful, we look for an outlet and shoot off toward some earthly idol—some counterfeit—rather than toward the one true living God. We commit spiritual adultery, which the Old Testament describes as harlotry; we embrace the bosom of another lover. But God wants us to fly to him, cling to him, run to him.

David Powlison says, "The occasions of a lust are never its cause. Temptations and sufferings do push our buttons, but they don't create those buttons."[2] As the pressure comes, and stuff is happening around you, you find yourself turning to certain things. And if you're not careful, you can think that the pressure created those things. But that button was already there—the pressure only revealed it.

How did the buttons get there? Who put them there? Raise your hand and say, "I did." Did you know you were doing it? Probably not, but the buttons are there just the same. James 1:14 explains, "But each one is tempted when he is drawn away by his own desires and enticed." The buttons were already there. The temptation came, the pressure came, the trial came, and a button was pushed. But you are the one who is responsible to remove the buttons—to repent of them.

The idolatrous buttons you create might be something like this: "I must be well thought of," "I must be popular," "I need attention," "I need people to think I'm attractive," "I need time to myself," "I must have a pain-free life," "I must keep looking young at all costs," "I must excel in sports," "I must be seen as a rising star at work," "I must retire early and comfortably," or "I must be free of financial worries." And you likely have many others and don't even know it. So the real battle begins by recognizing what your idols are. Living in ignorance of your idols is the primary reason you continue to struggle with particular sins.

PRESSURE COMES AT US FROM ALL SIDES

When my family lived in South Carolina, my brother-in-law helped me to install an inground sprinkler system in my front yard. I'd go out on the front porch and turn a little knob, and all around the yard, black plastic sprinkler heads would pop up. I never ran back into the house and said, "Kids, get out of bed! This is so cool! I turned this knob, and all these black plastic heads just popped up out of nowhere!" No—they had always been there. They were recessed in the ground, and it just took enough pressure, water pressure in this case, to run through the lines and pop them up.

The same is true with your heart. Your idols are recessed in your heart; you're just not aware of it. Then pressure comes, pops them up, and they do their thing, and you say, "Man, this is ugly. How did this happen? Where did this come from? Whoa!"

But the idols were there the whole time. And so God in his mercy brings pressure into our lives so that the idols can be exposed, and we can repent and really get free. So what are some of the pressures that God allows into our lives to expose the idols of our hearts?

Satan and All His Forces Are Bearing Down on You

First, you've got Satan and all his forces bearing down on you every day. First Peter 5:8 warns, "Be sober, be vigilant; because your adversary the devil walks about like a roaring lion, seeking whom he may devour." In Luke 22:31, Jesus told Peter, "Satan has asked for you." "Oh, great," you think—"Satan asks for me by name." Now, you might think yourself too insignificant for Satan to ask for you personally, but be assured that he or his minions are asking for you by name. "Satan has asked for you," Jesus said, "that he may sift you as wheat" (Luke 22:31). When workers sifted wheat in New Testament times, they would shake it violently to separate the chaff from the wheat.

That's what Satan wanted to do to Peter, and that's what he wants to do to you—shake you apart! So in the midst of trying to understand how the idols of your heart cause you to stumble into sin, remember that you also have a very real enemy. Along with the desires for pleasure that war in your members, don't ever forget, when you're squared off against a teenager, or a toddler, or your spouse, or your boss, or whoever, that above the fleshly zone there is a spiritual enemy who is doing all he can to shake you to pieces.

We're Suffering because We Live in a Broken World

We also have suffering because we live in a fallen world. In 1 Peter 4:12, Peter tells us not to be surprised: "Beloved, do not think it strange concerning the fiery trial which is to try you, as though some strange thing happened to you." Jesus said in John 16:33, "These things I have spoken to you, that in Me you may have peace. In the world you will have tribulation; but be of good cheer, I have overcome the world." That verse tells us two things about us right now as we walk the earth. The good news is that if you're a Christian, you are in Christ. The bad news is that although you are in Christ, you are also in the world, and in the world you will have tribulation.

It doesn't say, "Get ready—some of you might run into trouble." No, the Bible says that in the world you *will* have tribulation. I look forward to the day when only the first of those phrases will remain true. We'll be in Christ, in his presence, in heaven—removed from suffering, tribulation, and anguish. But for now we are both in Christ and in the world, so get ready to suffer. But take comfort, knowing that our suffering is used by God to expose our idols.

Your Own Sin Keeps Tripping You Up

So you've got Satan bearing down on you, and you've got suffering. Third, you have your own sin to deal with. Proverbs 5:22 says, "His own iniquities entrap the wicked man, and he is caught in the cords of his sin." We get caught up in the tangled web of our own sin.

That's why Hebrews 12:1–2 tells us to "lay aside every weight, and the sin which so easily ensnares us, and let us run with endurance the race that is set before us, looking unto Jesus, the author and finisher of our faith, who for the joy that was set before Him endured the cross, despising the shame, and has sat down at the right hand of the throne of God." Lay aside your sin. Watch out. Be alert. Hebrews 3 says, "Look out among you. Be on guard. Look out so that none of you falls captive to the deceitfulness of sin and the hardening of your heart that will turn you away from God" (Heb. 3:12–13 paraphrase).

Other People Keep Sinning against You

Not only is your own sin trying to entangle you, but you're surrounded by other sinful people as well. You live with a sinner spouse, trying to raise sinner kids, working for a sinner boss, living next door to sinner neighbors.

We need to remember that. We tend to forget, and then we're surprised when someone sins against us, which shows that we were trusting in that person too much to start with. I'm not saying that you should trust no one, or that you shouldn't open yourself up to others. What I'm pressing for is this: Where do you put your trust? What do you cling to? What is your hope invested in?

Let's say that you've had a rocky marriage, but with counseling it's starting to improve—your husband is beginning to repent. Don't start trusting in your marriage for all your happiness. Continue to trust God, and thank him for what he's doing in your husband, but don't redirect your trust away from God. When your marriage was bad, when you were desperate, you cried out to God, trusting him. And as your marriage improves, if you're not careful, you can slowly shift your trust from God to your husband. That is idolatry, and God will frustrate it and surprise you with a fresh reminder of your husband's sinfulness. We're not to trust in any human being. As Psalm 118:8–9 reminds us, "It is better to trust in the Lord than to put confidence in man. It is better to trust in the Lord than to put confidence in princes."

Jeremiah 17:5–8 says:

> Cursed is the man who trusts in man
> And makes flesh his strength,
> Whose heart departs from the Lord.

For he shall be like a shrub in the desert,
And shall not see when good comes,
But shall inhabit the parched places in the wilderness,
In a salt land which is not inhabited.

Blessed is the man who trusts in the LORD,
And whose hope is the LORD.
For he shall be like a tree planted by the waters,
Which spreads out its roots by the river,
And will not fear when heat comes;
But its leaf will be green,
And will not be anxious in the year of drought,
Nor will cease from yielding fruit.

Whenever you shift your trust from your Savior to other people, get ready for desert times—get ready to be parched, disillusioned, and disappointed. Don't do it!

Physical Sickness or Disease Takes Its Toll

Physical sickness can move into your life unexpectedly and suddenly—the body that was once able to do incredible feats begins the painful process of shutting down. The body that you could—years ago—push to the limits, and beyond, now refuses to respond the way you want it to. The body that required only three or four hours of sleep a night is now demanding far more attention than you ever imagined.

Sadly, at forty-nine years old, I'm there already. I never used to think about my body. I just had one. I was grateful for it and used it, but now when I wake up in the morning, wanting to hear a word from the Lord, the first thing I hear is my body talking to me. "Which part today?" I wonder. "Is it my Achilles' heel? My hip? My ears? My head? My . . . ?" And I'm not even fifty yet!

As you age, you can become consumed with your body and its latest illness—how you can't seem to shake it or find a medical solution. It gets frustrating, discouraging, even depressing. And if you're not careful, you're tempted to run to a false refuge, telling yourself, "I deserve a little pleasure. I deserve a little relief. I deserve a little break. I deserve something besides this constant pain."

You're Surrounded by Outside Pressure

Finally, as if that weren't enough, we have the all-purpose general category of outside pressure. Paul talks about it in 2 Corinthians 7:5: "our bodies had no rest, but we were troubled on every side. Outside were conflicts, inside were fears." Some days you feel that way—outside conflicts, inside fears. Second Corinthians 1:8–9, just a few chapters before, says that "we were burdened beyond measure, above strength, so that we despaired even of life. Yes, we had the sentence of death in ourselves"—why?—"that we should not trust in ourselves but in God who raises the dead."

RUNNING TO A REFUGE

Under pressure the heart becomes exposed, and it's a compass that shows where you run for refuge. The needle begins to quiver and move, and that pressure exposes the places where you run for cover.

Earlier I mentioned how God began to put his finger on my life as my wife and I went for help with our marriage; it was not going well, and it was characterized by conflict, wars, and fighting. We didn't physically hurt each other, but it was war nonetheless. There had to be a winner and a loser, and we both thought, "I'm going to win; you're going to lose."

When I was single and living with my parents in Knoxville, I read biographies about Jim Elliot and other missionaries; I had

Scripture verses pasted all over my desk and walls. I was working with the youth and playing my guitar and singing for Jesus, unaware of what a wretch I was. I thought I was a good guy—that some lucky woman was going to hit the jackpot with me. I worked construction during the day, and then came home exhausted. I would shower, gulp down supper, and go to my room to read biographies, pore over mission books, and pray. I mean, who wouldn't want a man like me? Women should have been beating down my door.

But I'll never forget one evening when my mom knocked on the door. She stuck her head in and said, "Bradley, I just want you to know that when you get married, you can't do this." And I remember sitting there thinking, "You've got to be kidding. What would need to change? This is all good stuff. I'm not mainlining drugs, Mom. I'm not snorting anything off my desk. There's no pornography in here. What are you talking about?" But my mother, who knew me well, realized that there was a selfish, me-centered heart in the body that was sitting there, surrounded by missionary biographies, Scripture verses, and posters about prayer. Because basically Brad Bigney did what Brad Bigney wanted to do when he wanted to do it for as long as he wanted to do it. And Mom could see a train wreck coming.

But of course, I didn't repent. My mom gave no details about what I was doing wrong—that was just her little "mother'" word, a little nugget that mothers give their sons—but it came back to me later. Three or four years into our marriage when everything hit the fan, I realized, "So that's what she was talking about!"

PRESSURE EXPOSES OUR IDOLS

I couldn't see my own sin and my own idols—and neither can you most of the time. But God designs exactly what is needed to expose them, all in his time. As the pressure came into my life with a wife, two little kids, a tiny trailer, an old car, seminary, the demands of a new church (leading worship and working with the students), I kept going harder and harder, thinking, "I have to do it all."

As the pressure increased, along with the friction in my marriage and family, the refuge I ran to the most was the church. I thought I could just work harder at my job. The marriage thing I didn't understand. I didn't get it at all. Vicki had liked me when we dated, but I could tell that she didn't like me anymore. So I set about finding other people who *did* like me. I knew my marriage was in deep weeds, but I didn't have the time or the inclination to sort it out. It made no sense to me—we just kept having the same conversations over and over. So I thought, "Enough of this! I'm out of here! I'll go build the Easter tomb. I'll rent the smoke machine. We'll have a gurney lift Jesus for the ascension this year at the Easter musical. Bigger, better, *more*!"

I was more comfortable, and felt more capable, when I was serving at church, so I did even more. "I can please these people," I thought. And the strokes—ah, yes, the strokes! People said, "Oh, you're the best pastor we've ever had." And that was some consolation as I continued to get nothing but a steady dose of nagging, criticism, and silence at home.

But the pressure had to increase—more and more—for the idols to be exposed. And as painful as it was, as confusing as it was to Vicki and me, it was the most merciful thing that God could have done—bringing enough pressure into our lives to make those little sprinkler heads pop up, so that we could identify and start putting to death the idols of our hearts that had been driving us.

Too often, however, the first recourse under pressure is not to repent of the idols, but to run somewhere else. I don't know what it is like in your life. Maybe you're under pressure right now, with Satan, suffering, sickness, your own sin, other people's sin, or outside pressure. But let me encourage you not to run anywhere but to God. Tell him, "God, this hurts; this is such a mess. God, I'm confused. What do you want to expose in me? What do you want me to see about my own heart that I'm not seeing? I'm ready to repent."

Money

For you, it might be money. When you're afraid, you look to the idol of money to give you security. You don't want it to rule you; you just want it to give you those things that the world says will anchor your life—a certain home, or car, or vacation, or lifestyle.

Pleasure

For some, the refuge is pleasure. When the pressure is on, you look for quick gratification. "I just need a hit of pleasure," you tell yourself. This is where pornography comes in. Not everyone who is ensnared in pornography is a sex addict. You might be a pleasure addict. You just want quick, intense self-focus, so that you don't have to give, or worry about a relationship with someone else. Pornographic pleasure is false intimacy.

Food

Food is a refuge for others. Whether through bulimia, anorexia, or gluttony, it's an abuse of both the stomach and the appetites. Maybe you crave the pleasure that food provides so badly that you can't give it up, can't stop, no matter how obese you become. If you want badly enough not to get fat, or if you want to control the effects of how much you are eating, you vomit it back up. But be sure of this—an idol is ruling your heart. You want so badly to be in control—of something—that you control your food intake until you starve yourself to death.

Whatever

Your refuge might be sleep, or shopping, or entertainment—maybe you just disappear into the world of TV, movies, video games, or the Internet. Whatever your refuge looks like, it's what Paul is talking about in Philippians 3:18–19 when he says:

> For many walk, of whom I have told you often, and now tell you even weeping, that they are the enemies of the cross of Christ: whose end is destruction, whose god is their belly [appetites, pleasure, desires], and whose glory is in their shame—who set their mind on earthly things.

When we go anywhere else except to God himself, we make ourselves enemies of the cross of Christ; we disdain the cross of Christ; we turn from the cross of Christ and say, "No, no, no. It's somewhere else. I'll find refuge and satisfaction somewhere else."

That is the essence of idolatry—setting your mind on earthly things. David Powlison makes this observation:

> I remember the time I counseled a man who habitually escaped life's pressures into TV, food, video games, alcohol, pornography, antique collecting, sci-fi novels. Where to begin? Could I find a passage to focus his problems? I wasn't sure what to pick up on. Then it struck me. Try the Psalms—as a whole! Almost every single Psalm, in some way or other, portrays the Lord as our refuge in trouble. The Psalms implicitly and explicitly rebuke taking refuge in anything less; the Psalms offer steadfast love and mercy; the Psalms spur us to know and obey God in the trenches of life. This man felt vaguely guilty for some of his bad behavior. But he didn't see the

pattern or the seriousness. His efforts at change were half-baked and unsuccessful. Conviction of the specific sin of his heart—turning from the living God in order to seek idolatrous refuge—woke him up, and made him see his behavioral sins in a fresh way. He even began to identify little escapist tricks he hadn't even realized he did—ways he misused humor or made subtle excuses for himself. Christ's grace became very real and necessary. He became motivated to practical change—to face pressures and responsibilities to God's glory.[3]

GOD WON'T HELP THOSE WHO DESERT HIM

Pressure attacks us from all sides, and when it does we're tempted to run somewhere for a refuge, and we quickly find out that God won't help those who desert him. He won't help those who, while serving their idols, expect him to *help them serve them*. You keep clinging to your idols, and even while you're praying and fasting, you're saying, "God, I just need this, and if you were good, you'd give it to me."

But God won't help you to serve your idols.

Jonah 2:8 teaches, "Those who cling to worthless idols forfeit the grace that could be theirs" (NIV). God is telling you, "I'll help you. I've got grace for you. There is a way through this problem of yours, but I'll see that you don't find it as long as you hang on to your idols."

What about you? Is the pressure on? If so, what is the compass of your heart revealing? Where's the needle pointing? If it's anyplace other than God, pray, "God, the pressure's on. I need *you*. I'm coming to *you* even more, God." What you're clinging to is a dead end, a dry well, a counterfeit. It *will* disappoint you, guaranteed. Make God your refuge. Not anyone else, not anything else.

Only God.

HOMEWORK

Think through the pressures that are in your life right now. God wants those pressures to drive you to him! Take time to read, meditate, and even memorize some of the Scriptures below that speak of God's being your refuge. Take the verses and write your own prayer from them. Finally, write down what you think your idols might be, based on where you run to under pressure, and lay them down. Repent.

God is in the idol-smashing business not because he's egotistical. He's in the idol-smashing business because he is *good*, and because he's good, he knows you'll never find happiness in counterfeits. They will lead only to more messes and further entanglements if you go anywhere but to him. He would prove himself unloving, ungracious, and unmerciful if he let you go. For his glory and our good, he's in the idol-smashing business.

The following verses are a good place to start as you learn about God as a refuge. Think about, memorize, and pray through these Scriptures:

> The eternal God is your refuge,
> And underneath are the everlasting arms. (Deut. 33:27)
>
> In you, O LORD, I put my trust;
> Let me never be ashamed;
> Deliver me in Your righteousness.
> Bow down Your ear to me,
> Deliver me speedily;
> Be my rock of refuge,
> A fortress of defense to save me.
>
> For You are my rock and my fortress;
> Therefore, for Your name's sake,

Lead me and guide me.
Pull me out of the net which they have secretly laid for me,
For You are my strength.
Into Your hand I commit my spirit;
You have redeemed me, O Lord God of truth.

I have hated those who regard useless idols;
But I trust in the Lord.
I will be glad
    and rejoice in your mercy,
For You have considered my trouble;
You have known my soul in adversities. (Ps. 31:1–7)

God is our refuge and strength,
A very present help in trouble.
. . . .

Be still, and know that I am God;
I will be exalted among the nations,
I will be exalted in the earth!

The Lord of hosts is with us;
The God of Jacob is our refuge. (Ps. 46:1, 10–11)

For indeed, those who are far from You shall perish;
You have destroyed all those who desert You for harlotry.
But it is good for me to draw near to God;
I have put my trust in the Lord God,
That I may declare all Your works. (Ps. 73:27–28)

CHAPTER 11

LET GOD BE GOD!

An idol is anything or anyone that begins to capture our hearts, minds, and affections more than God.

In chapter 5 we looked at how, when ensnared in the trap of idolatry, we take on a new identity. It's not simply that you're clinging to a counterfeit refuge. Idolatry changes who you think you are, how you see yourself. You adopt a new persona as you worship at the altar of your own idols, and given enough time, you'll start to redefine yourself in terms of those idols.

"I AM MY OWN REDEEMER": DEFINING YOURSELF BY YOUR OWN PERFORMANCE IN THE CHRISTIAN LIFE

And that redefinition of how you see yourself leads to one of the most deadly counterfeits, and yet it is one of the most prevalent identity replacements we face today. As a pastor—and a sinner myself—I run into this twisted identity regularly, as I'm trying to help people who are snared in sin. It's the trap of "I am my own redeemer."

Make no mistake, nobody wearing the *evangelical Christian* label has ever walked up to me and said, "Check it out; I'm my own redeemer." Most Christians have enough theological savvy to steer clear of that. But I see it all the time—the same Christians who get fired up about "salvation by grace alone" will deftly set it aside, thinking they can live the Christian life in their own strength. They'd never say it with their lips, but with their life they're saying, "I needed a redeemer for salvation—to get out of the starting blocks—but now it's all about how hard I can work to please God, finding out what he says to do and then doing it!" It's basically an attitude of "Thanks for getting me started, Jesus, but I can take it from here." And though they're armed with solid biblical principles, surrounded by fellow believers, and in a Bible-believing church, sooner or later the wheels fall off, and they either self-destruct or end up as spiritual killjoys—cranky, tired, and unhappy. They lose steam, lose their joy, and wonder what went wrong, searching—along with hordes of other spiritual casualties—for some biblical "secret," some panacea that will get them "back in the zone" spiritually.

Counselor and author Leslie Vernick observes that this struggle is so prevalent because we don't really understand grace or fully embrace the gospel. We really don't. We sing about it and keep it in our creeds and on our bumper stickers, but slowly, like some giant Norwegian cruise ship, we begin doing a 180 back in the direction of law and self-effort. Referring to one of her counselees, Vernick relates:

> As I got to know Kaitlyn more, I found that she habitually fretted over her sins, flaws and imperfections, both real and imagined. When we, like Kaitlyn, are morbidly introspective or self-conscious, we turn in on ourself, analyzing and examin-

> ing, always trying to explain, understand, or make sense out of our lives. We become our own Holy Spirit, gazing inward, looking for flaws, and usually finding them.
>
> Gary Thomas rightly suggests that when we are constantly anxious about or disappointed with ourselves, perhaps we have made an "idol out of our own piety." To grow into the person God wants us to be, we need to die to our habit of constantly gazing at ourselves, being morbidly occupied, worried, and anxious about our performance or lack of perfection. Instead, we need to learn to take our eyes off ourselves and fix them on the perfection, beauty, and grace of God.[1]

That's why the apostolic writer said this in Hebrews 12:2: "looking unto Jesus, the author and finisher of our faith." Most Christians are conscious of Jesus as the author of our faith. But the church of Jesus Christ, and Christians at large, are weak in their understanding of Jesus as the finisher. Jesus starts it *and* he finishes it.

That's a message that needs to be shouted up and down the aisles of our churches today. You didn't start it, and you can't finish it. Oh, how freeing that would be for most Christians today, and how robust the church of Jesus Christ would look if his children were feasting on the good news of the gospel and all its implications, instead of marching in their own strength to the drumbeat of "We Try Harder!"

We forget that he's the perfecter, and so we spin our spiritual wheels, trying to perfect ourselves.

Sound familiar? Are you focused on the perfectionistic standards that you've set for yourself and those around you? Are you overcritical and judgmental, both of yourself and of others? Are you morbidly introspective—do you regularly comb through your life in microscopic detail? Then you might be one of these evangelical "I am my own redeemer" types, and don't even know it.

Now let me ask you a question that can flush out the "I am my own redeemer" type. In your Christian theology, do you have any place for the sins of true saints? Do you know what I'm asking? In other words, what do you do with sin? You see, people who love God, know God, and are saved still sin. Surprised? You shouldn't be. Maybe you'd say, "Sure. I know Christians still sin—the Bible talks about that." Okay, but I'm asking you what you do with that sin. How does it play out in your life?

Here's why I'm pressing you on this—because what I'm seeing more and more is believers who become immobilized after they sin. They end up treading spiritual water for weeks, months, or even years, with Satan right there beating them up, so that there's no joy, no peace, and no direction in their lives. And because of that, they're useless for God. They're so bogged down with morbid introspection—beating themselves up over their sin—that when they lose their temper with their kids again, they can't even confess it. They can't get over it and move on. And Satan smiles and says, "I've got you just where I want you."

So let me ask you again—is there anyplace in your Christian life for recognizing that you are going to sin? There had better be.

I'm not saying to get excited about sinning, or to get up each morning and compile a to-do list of all the sins you are going to commit. Don't plan to sin. Plan to go hard after God; set your sights on pleasing him; pray that he will fill you with the Holy Spirit; put on the armor of God; read your Bible. But know ahead of time that there won't be a single day between now and eternity in which you won't sin at some point.

So what do you do when you sin? What do you think, and where do you run after you've sinned? So many Christians lack good, biblical answers for that question, and it's robbing them of joy and usefulness in God's kingdom because they get bogged down and waste time beating themselves up every time they sin. Instead of running to the cross and soaking again in the marvelous light of the gospel, they sit mired in their own perfectionistic standards, bemoaning the fact that they failed again. Remember this: your failure is never a surprise to God. That's why Christ died.

Again Leslie Vernick says:

> There are those who have been morbidly introspective and self-conscious their entire lives. They are fearful, anxious, and insecure because they not only over-examine themselves, but do so with a microscope. The problem with these folks is that their measuring rod is their own idealized version of their perfect self, not God's Word. Oswald Chambers cautioned us when he said, "I am called to live in perfect relation to God so that my life produces a longing after God in other lives, not admiration for myself. Thoughts about myself hinder my usefulness to God. God is not after perfecting me to be a specimen in His showroom; He is getting me to the place where He can use me."[2]

People who live under the weight of a self-made perfectionistic standard are constantly thinking about themselves. They're so consumed with measuring themselves that there's no time to fix their eyes on Christ, and so there's precious little energy and emotion left over to invest in the kingdom by serving, loving, and thinking of others.

Maybe I'm describing you. Maybe you've spent the bulk of your Christian life grooming yourself to be a specimen in God's showroom, and vacillating wildly back and forth between fresh starts of pursuing holiness and self-flagellation for failing again and again. Get the gospel back into focus in your life. Christ came and died for us while we were helpless, hopeless, weak sinners. God delights in using broken and far-from-perfect sinners whom he has saved by his grace for his glory.

Maybe you're thinking, "That's not what I heard growing up in church." Have you ever heard a preacher or other well-meaning Christian say, "God won't use a dirty vessel"?

Well, there's a lot that I still don't understand about the Bible, but after reading it from cover to cover, year after year, I do have an answer for the "God won't use a dirty vessel" messengers.

Poppycock.

That's right, *poppycock*. A Dutch word meaning "waste," "rubbish," or "fecal matter."

If God never used a dirty vessel, he'd never use anybody! But praise God, dirty vessels are all he has to work with. Read your Bible! It's filled with people who were less-than-perfect poster children for the cause of God, but God used them anyway.

Matthew 1:1–17 is the genealogy of Christ, and it's a billboard of grace that puts on display the very point that I'm trying to make here. The Holy Spirit included in this list three women that we would have found some way to skip over or sweep under the rug: Tamar (v. 3), Rahab (v. 5), and "her who had been the wife of Uriah" (v. 6). Now, if you're new to the Bible, let me help you out. Verse 6 is talking about Bathsheba. She was the wife of Uriah, but had sex with the sweet psalmist, David. Shocking, I know.

So who were these women? Bathsheba was an adulteress. Rahab was a prostitute. And Tamar *pretended* to be a prostitute in order to have sex with her father-in-law (I don't have time to go into it all, but it's ugly—and you can read all about it in Genesis chapter 38—and let's just say that it doesn't usually get you on the list of "Who's Who"). And some of you thought you had a bad relationship with your father-in-law; tricking your father-in-law into having sex with you as a prostitute really puts a strain on the holidays and family get-togethers.

But here's my point. These women are included in this genealogy because God wants us to be swallowed up in the wideness of his grace and mercy. His grace and mercy are not a puddle, not a pond, but a bottomless ocean vast and deep. So no one reading these words is beyond the reach of God's grace. No matter what you've done, where you've been, or what's been done to you, God's grace is greater. His kingdom has room for you as an adopted son or daughter, and he has a seat for you at his banquet table of grace. Isn't that good?

I don't know what you're going through. I don't know what you're feeling. And I don't know what you're thinking. But I want you to know that our God is the God of Tamar, the God of Rahab, and the God of Bathsheba. Our God is in the business of shining his glory through broken vessels that this world would toss out onto the trash heap as useless. He delights in picking up the broken shards and making us into trophies of grace for the display of his glory.

That's why the apostle Paul observed that "where sin abounded, grace abounded much more" (Rom. 5:20). And he knew that the same thing was true about himself when he said, "But by the grace of God I am what I am, and His grace toward me was not in vain; but I labored more abundantly than they all, yet not I, but the grace of God which was with me" (1 Cor. 15:10). Paul drives it home further in his second letter to the Corinthians:

> For we do not preach ourselves, but Christ Jesus the Lord, and ourselves your bondservants for Jesus' sake. For it is the God who commanded light to shine out of darkness, who has shone in our hearts to give the light of the knowledge of the glory

> of God in the face of Jesus Christ. But we have this treasure in earthen vessels, that the excellence of the power may be of God and not of us. (2 Cor. 4:5–7)

God delights in using people with a past.

But what about the present? What about the day-to-day failures and shortcomings that leave us feeling like so much less than conquerors? In the midst of your struggles, in the midst of your falling short, in the midst of your fighting against sin and falling yet again, God can still use you. He can still use you to witness to your neighbor, even after you bite the heads off your children for their fighting and bickering. He can do that. Is he pleased with the head-biting-off moment? No, but that doesn't disqualify you from being used by him, because the Christian life is not some kind of merit system. God never says, "Oh, you just ripped your kids' heads off, so I can't use you now. You'll have no words. You'll have no thoughts. You won't remember Romans 3:23. You can't share the gospel." Thankfully, God hasn't set up that sort of works-based system. He is a God of grace—grace for salvation, and grace for daily Christian living.

But we so easily fall back into thinking, "Uh-oh, I did it again, so I might have a car wreck on the way to work today," or "I hit the snooze button and missed my quiet time," or "I'm twenty-one days behind in my Bible-reading plan. Surely God is about to hit the 'Smite' button in my life."

We might know intellectually that this sort of thinking does not reflect truth, but we begin to feel and live as though it did. The "I am my own redeemer" idol is hamstringing so many Christians today who would wave the "Saved by grace" party banner, but who then turn around and try to live the Christian life in their own strength.

Here's the real problem: If you battle with this kind of thinking, you probably have too high an opinion of yourself. Ugly pride is what's lurking behind the mask of "I am my own redeemer." Pride is a huge factor with perfectionistic, performance-driven people. They're so devastated when they fall short of their standards (not just God's!) because they think so highly of themselves. Instead of recognizing that they can do nothing apart from Christ, they live their days focused on what they're trying to do. And they are only mildly—if at all—conscious of Jesus Christ living in them. And so there's no desperate, rock-bottom recognition that apart from Christ, they can't do anything. In fact, they actually think they can and should do a lot. That's why they're devastated when they fail.

So what's the answer? How do you climb out of the idolatry and false identity of "I am my own redeemer"? Let me give you some ways.

DON'T LET YOUR SPIRITUAL DISCIPLINES DEGENERATE INTO RAW REGULATIONS INSTEAD OF A LIVING RELATIONSHIP WITH CHRIST

By *spiritual disciplines,* I mean Bible reading, prayer, worship, witnessing, journaling, silence and solitude, fasting, serving, giving, and more. All of these are great disciplines, and God encourages us to make good use of them. But here's the danger: before you know it, what started off as a journey of grace begins to narrow into the cramped, dark tunnel of your own performance. And it shuts the window on grace. The Christian life starts feeling stuffy—there's no joy, no sense of freedom, because the sunshine of God's grace is crowded out by the dark clouds of performance and spiritual duties.

All the while, God is saying, "Stop! I saved you by grace while you were an enemy, while you were hostile, while you were a wretch. I love you. Our relationship is based on grace and the cross and Christ, not on what you can do for me now."

So should you throw out the spiritual disciplines? Should you give up trying to fast, read your Bible, and pray? No; just do them with a new motive. The purpose of spiritual disciplines is to know God better and to experience communion with him, not to earn his favor. For the believer, God's favor is yours every day, based on Christ and his righteousness, not on anything that you're doing or not doing.

Pastor C. J. Mahaney describes this dilemma well in *The Cross Centered Life*:

> Meet Stuart. He's a brand-new Christian. He has a lot to learn about the Christian life, but he has a genuine love for Jesus Christ. One Sunday morning during the church service, his friend Mike notices that Stuart has a little trouble finding the book of Romans. After the meeting, he comes over to Stuart and asks him if he's regularly reading his Bible. "Uh, sure," Stuart replies. "There's so much there, I just look at different things." Mike raises his eyebrows, "You're reading at random? That's really not the best way. You need to read the Word seriously. Listen, I have this schedule that tells you how to read the whole Bible in a year, a little every day. I'll make you a copy." "Wow!" Stuart says. "You mean by this time next year I could have read the entire Bible? That would be great!" And so just a few days later, Stuart places a single flexible rod onto the stage of his Christian life, lifts up a plate called Bible Reading and gives it a hard spin. And it stays in place.
>
> After Mike told him about the importance of Bible reading, Jimmy encouraged him to meditate on Scripture, Andrew extolled the glories of attending a weekly accountability meet-

> ing with guys from the church, and in a sermon, his pastor emphasized the importance of church prayer meetings. Then Stuart attended a conference on evangelism. He needed to be witnessing every day. Then he heard a radio program about fasting and another about personal holiness. One by one, Stuart added more and more spiritual activities to his life. Each was good. Some were vital. Yet without realizing it, Stuart allowed a dangerous shift to take place in his mind and heart. What God had intended to be a means of experiencing grace, Stuart had changed into a means of earning grace. Instead of being a further expression of his confidence in God's saving work in his life, his spiritual activities became spinning plates to maintain.
>
> The shift is plainly seen on Sunday mornings. On one Sunday, Stuart sings and praises God with evident sincerity and zeal. Why? Because he's just had a really good week; not a single plate has wobbled. But on another Sunday, following a week in which several plates fell, Stuart is hesitant to approach God. He finds it difficult to worship freely, because he feels that God disapproves of him. His confidence is no longer in the gospel; it's in his own performance, which hasn't been so great lately.[3]

Does Stuart's life describe yours? Be honest. Where is your confidence? Is it in the gospel, or in your own performance of spiritual duties? Is it hard for you to enter into worship because you're conscious of certain spiritual "plates" that have fallen in the past week? Do you have to do a "plate check" every time you get ready to approach God? Is your ability to come into his presence based on your spinning plates, or on Christ's finished work?

If you're depending on spinning plates, it won't be long before your Christian joy gets sucked out of your life, leaving in its place a suffocating, I-don't-think-I-can-keep-doing-all-this-forever depression. The abundant life turns into the redundant list, as the promises of Christ's abundant life in you become choked by the redundant list of regulations that you've created in order to redeem yourself.

When they're functioning as they should, the spiritual disciplines, rather than suffocating you, will strengthen your relationship with God. But maybe you're thinking, "What's the difference between making wise use of spiritual disciplines and falling into the idolatrous trap of performance for self?" It has to do with the motivation behind what you're doing. Self-performance says, "I'll do these things to gain good standing with God." Godly discipline says, "I'll do these things because I love God, I want to know him better, and I want to experience more of his grace. And I'll do it knowing that he could never love me more than he already does, because I am in Christ!"

SOAK IN THE SCRIPTURES AS THOUGH YOU WERE READING THEM FOR THE VERY FIRST TIME

One of the best ways to do this is to get yourself a clean, new Bible. It doesn't have to be expensive, just clean—no highlights, underlining, or other marks—so that you won't be influenced by something you wrote before. The object is for you to read it as though for the first time.

Recently I had the oil changed in my car. As I sat in the waiting area with a crisp, clean New American Standard Bible in my lap, I was reading 1 Peter 4 and had a sudden, wonderful, and unexpected moment of worship, despite the cigarette smoke and country music that filled the waiting area. Reading a clean page of 1 Peter chapter 4, I pondered verses I'd read many times before, some of which I'd even tried to memorize, but it was marvelous to see the chapter again in a fresh, new way.

I recommend that you start with the book of Galatians. Read it carefully and prayerfully, because the entire book exalts the grace of God that is ours through the cross of Christ. For six chapters, Paul is on a rampage to defend the very heart of the gospel, and to remind us that Christ is our Redeemer—not our works, not our efforts, and certainly not our spinning plates.

For example, look at Galatians 3:3: "Are you so foolish? Having begun in the Spirit, are you now being made perfect by the flesh?" Paul had already given the Galatians the gospel himself, but they soon fell into the trap of trying to live the Christian life by their own efforts. So Paul reminds them, "Are you trying to perfect in the flesh what was started by the Spirit?" He says, "Are you so foolish?" God began his work in us—by the Spirit—and it can be perfected only by God, by his Spirit. It's the Spirit dwelling within you that enables you to live the Christian life, not your tenacious pursuit of the spiritual disciplines.

REFUSE TO LEAVE YOUR SAVIOR BEHIND!

I know that might sound basic, but it needs to be stated. In fact, you might need to look back over your shoulder and recognize that that speck in the distance is your Savior. You were meant to live the Christian life walking *with* your Savior, in communion *with* your Savior, delighting *in* your Savior, trusting *in* your Savior, not marching on courageously in your own strength. But here's what happens, especially in a church that has a high view of God's Word. You are taught to go to Scripture for biblical principles relating to marriage, parenting, finances, idols of the heart, pride, and so on. So far, so good. But, depraved sinners that we are, we seek ways to boil everything down to a few principles. We create a system or a checklist that we can work on in our own strength.

But God didn't design the Christian life to be boiled down to a checklist. If he had, the Bible could be a very small, indexed book, with all the handy checklists for pride under *P*, and anger under *A*, and sexual sin under *S*. Instead, he composed the Bible largely in narrative form, because he intended the Bible to draw us into relationship with *him*, not to serve as a system that we can take and run with on our own. Otherwise, we wouldn't need God at all.

GET RID OF YOUR "CHECKLIST" MENTALITY

Living by a checklist won't work—not for long, anyway. And the time you spend on it just wears you out—not to mention everyone around you! In John 15:5, Jesus proclaims, "I am the vine, you are the branches. He who abides in Me, and I in him, bears much fruit; for without Me you can do nothing." Maybe you've been trying to live the Christian life without him, wondering why you feel so spiritually exhausted and uptight all the time. Check yourself—see whether you've got a checklist clenched in your spiritual fist, as you white-knuckle the steering wheel of the Christian life. If that's you, then you're in for a crash, because biblical principles—divorced from the Savior who designed them—can never produce the results you're looking for. You can knock yourself out and work-work-work-work-work, but it will never fill the void left by the absence of a living, loving, joyful relationship with Christ.

Christian counselor Wayne Brown says, "I am similarly convinced that trust in the security of Christian principles is being confused with faith in God."[4] As a parent, you can be drawn in to gathering all the biblical principles you can find that speak to parenting, and then trust in *them*, instead of God, to transform your child's heart. If you're not careful, you'll turn parenting into sweat equity, thinking, "If I put all these parenting principles into practice, I'm guaranteed to have godly kids." Watch out! That way of thinking usually ends in heartache and disappointment, with you pressing on—miserable but diligent—pretending that the system is working when it's not.

You can't trust in principles. You absolutely have to trust in God *alone*.

Trusting in principles makes you feel as though you're in control. It puts you in the driver's seat of your Christian life, and we all love to be in control. Trusting God leaves you . . . well, trusting God, and that's especially hard in areas that are as dear to you as your kids. Christian counselor Wayne Brown remarks:

> The impulse to control—to get it all lined up—is often a manifestation of fear, not faith. We might pump up the principles and send them floating overhead like a Goodyear blimp with the words "Right Christian Living" branded bold and tall on its shimmering skin. But the fiery sparks of real life always bring it back to earth, sometimes in a nose dive, Hindenburg fashion. The beguiled Christians, falling from the spiritual dirigible as it tilts, groans and bursts into flames, often land on my couch. "Why didn't it work?" they ask. "Right Christian Living was supposed to keep me aloft, freed from my childhood hurt, rising above my bent toward sin, successful in my marriage and employment." I usually wait a few sessions before suggesting that perhaps the ship's pilot was someone other than God. It didn't work, I then tell them, because principles—Christian or not—will always fail you. At some point your decency will spring a leak. Your good parenting will buckle under the weight of human frailty. The shocking

> crack in your best intentions will reveal a darker motive. You have been looking to these things to save you, not guide you. Sometimes they understand this. Sometimes they don't. And sometimes they ask for a book on how to get the blimp up and running again.[5]

What about you? Maybe your blimp of "Right Christian Living" crashed, leaving you bitter and miserable. Know this: even in the smoldering wreckage, you can get back to where you should have been all along—looking to God, depending on him, enjoying him, and delighting in his gospel.

The Christian life is all about Christ. Philippians 3:3 says, "For we are the circumcision, who worship God in the Spirit, rejoice in Christ Jesus, and have no confidence in the flesh." Our confidence has to be in God and Jesus Christ. Paul continues, "[I want to] be found in Him, not having my own righteousness, which is from the law, but that which is through faith in Christ, the righteousness which is from God by faith" (Phil. 3:9). *The Message* paraphrase puts it this way: "I didn't want some petty, inferior brand of righteousness that comes from keeping a list of rules when I could get the robust kind that comes from trusting Christ—*God's* righteousness."

REFOCUS AND BALANCE YOUR PRAYERS

Often we don't pray rightly. Our prayers are lopsided, leaning too much toward ourselves and our sin. Don't get me wrong—confession of sin is essential. But true confession is to agree with God and say, "I've sinned." But God isn't a despot who loves to watch us wallow at his feet, beating ourselves up after we've confessed our sin to him. Rather, he loves to see us worship. And that happens best when we keep our eyes focused on our Savior and his work on the cross rather than our sin.

The Puritans had the right balance—they understood how to pray. They didn't minimize their sin; they took it seriously, and they took pursuing God seriously. But they never drifted far from the cross, from grace, or from their Savior. They didn't wallow in their failures or mourn over their sins. They beat a path to the cross and rejoiced in it. They understood the need for living a cross-centered life.

The Puritan prayer below is an example of what I'm talking about:

> O Lord,
> Bend my hands and cut them off,
> for I have often struck thee with a wayward will,
> when these fingers should embrace thee by faith.
> I am not yet weaned from all created glory,
> honor, wisdom and esteem of others,
> for I have a secret motive to eye my name in all I do.
> Let me not only speak the word sin, but see the thing itself.
> Give me to view a discovered sinfulness,
> to know that though my sins are crucified
> they are never wholly mortified.
> Hatred, malice, ill-will,
> vain-glory that hungers for and hunts after
> man's approval and applause,
> all are crucified, forgiven,
> but they rise again in my sinful heart.
> O my crucified but never wholly mortified sinfulness!
> O my life-long damage and daily shame!
> O my indwelling and besetting sins!
> O the tormenting slavery of a sinful heart!
> Destroy, O God, the dark guest within
> whose hidden presence makes my life a hell.
> Yet thou hast not left me here without grace;
> The cross still stands and meets my needs
> in the deepest straits of the soul. . . .

The memory of my great sins, my many temptations, my falls,
bring afresh into my mind the remembrance
of thy great help, of thy support from heaven,
of the great grace that saved such a wretch as I am.
There is no treasure so wonderful
as that continuous experience of thy grace towards me
which alone can subdue the risings of sin within:
Give me more of it.[6]

"Give me more of it—more of your grace!" That's how we need to pray and how we need to live. If you're guilty of living the Christian life in your own strength, cry out to God and say, "I want more of your continuous grace. I don't want to be stuck with my own cheap, inferior righteousness—I want the robust kind." Maybe you've never tasted the robust kind. Cry out for it! Maybe you don't know Christ at all. You're still a slave to sin. Cry out to him for mercy! Let this be the day you throw down the cheap, inferior brand of righteousness and begin smelling, tasting, delighting in, and clinging to the robust kind that is found in Christ alone.

Chapter 12

GOD'S PRESCRIPTION FOR FREEDOM

WHAT IS THE CURE FOR THE WANDERING HEART?

I hope by now you've identified some of your own idols. If not, stop right now—ask God to change you. Don't just read this book. Find out what's going on in your heart. Pray, "God, what idols are hanging me up in my own life? Where do I need to repent?" It's a tough thing, discerning what exactly is going on in your heart, isn't it? You may not be aware of what you're clinging to, what you're craving, and what you're worshiping instead of God. You're more conscious of the people in your way, the people you think need to change. So stop right now and take time to get quiet before God and focus on your heart.

Proverbs 20:5 observes, "Counsel in the heart of man is like deep water, but a man of understanding will draw it out." What's going on inside you—why you do what you do—is like deep water, and along with God's grace and the help of the Holy Spirit, you'll need a generous portion of understanding, humility, courage, and time to draw it out. I'm praying that this book will help you draw out and expose what's going on in your heart.

Once that happens, once God shows you what's going on inside you, what then? In this chapter, I want to introduce you to three habits that you need to establish in order to consistently detect and destroy idols of the heart.

HABIT #1: ESTABLISH AND MAINTAIN A WARTIME MENTALITY

Don't think of dealing with idols as a one-time event. Don't put this book down and say, "Okay, this is the year I destroy all the idols of my heart; once that's done, I can move on and focus on other areas of the Christian life." It doesn't work that way. This is a lifelong battle. You need to think in terms of the conflict between Israel and Palestine, which has gone on as long as I've been alive, rather than some skirmish—some blitzkrieg—like Operation Desert Storm back in the '90s. It's not a matter of just blasting the enemy once and for all in one fell swoop. The heart is a tireless machine, a twenty-four-hour factory of idols, and as fast as you smash one, your heart cranks out another. It never stops, never takes a break.

So dealing with idols is not for the faint of heart. It's messy and exhausting, and it never seems to be completely done. Until God delivers us from these fleshly bodies, the heart never fully surrenders. We sing "I Surrender All," but honestly, we don't have the capacity to maintain total surrender, especially not for every minute of every day for the rest of our lives. The heart never throws down its weapons because the flesh wars against the Spirit: "For the sinful nature desires what is contrary to the Spirit, and the Spirit what is contrary to the sinful nature. They are in conflict with each other, so that you do not do what you want" (Gal. 5:17 NIV).

That's not to say it's not worth the effort, not worth the fight. Parenting is also hard and exhausting and never completely done, but you wouldn't think of giving up on it just because you can't do it perfectly. The same is true of rooting out idols of the heart. But to do it successfully, you have to establish a wartime mentality, and you have to maintain it for the rest of your life. The good news is that God gives us everything we need to maintain that wartime mentality. He gives us his grace, his Holy Spirit, and his Word, along with the solid footing of the gospel to stand on. On top of that, he gives us direct access to his throne through prayer, and the help and encouragement of fellow believers to speak into our lives.

Keep in mind that you face an enemy who is skilled at all sorts of deceptive tactics, as in any earthly war. Idols hide and camouflage themselves, and they don't play by international rules of warfare. They rarely come out into the open, and when they do, they aren't wearing nametags such as "Hello, my name is Envy." Like some terrorist cell group, they hide out in the mountains of your heart and carry out covert operations while your attention is occupied elsewhere. And their faces change—they are masters of disguise, often disappearing only to resurface with new names, new identities, and new ways of gunning you down.

And they don't stay dead. You stab them again and again, and you drag their nasty carcasses around to make sure they're good and dead. But when you least expect it—at the most inopportune moment in your life—that idol you thought you'd dealt with will jump out from behind some corner in your heart and scare the fool out of you, getting your sinful adrenaline all ramped up again. That's what idols do. You might think you're safe, but you never are.

Idols are like chameleons, manifesting themselves in different ways, depending on your circumstances, your season of life, your age, your job, and your current struggles. And they manifest themselves differently, depending on where you're weakest at any given point in your life.

For example, 2 Timothy 3:4 talks about men and women who are "lovers of pleasure rather than lovers of God." So if you're struggling with the idol of pleasure, it can manifest itself in countless ways. That's why you can't just focus on the obvious or immediate problem. What does a "lover of pleasure" idol look like?

One way in which a "lover of pleasure" idol could manifest itself is by causing you to sit in front of a computer screen looking at pornography. And when God begins to convict you, you shut down the porn, only to replace it with gambling at the local casino, because it gives you the same rush and the same excitement.

Then, as your gambling debts pile up, friends step in and take your car keys so that you can't drive to the casino anymore, but then you find yourself back in front of the computer—not with porn, but with playing *Call of Duty* for hours on end, cutting down enemy soldiers because it provides not only a pleasurable escape from reality, but also immediate gratification. And no other area of your life feels that way—not your marriage, not your job.

But your wife complains about the time you're wasting in front of the computer instead of talking to her and the kids, so you turn off the computer, only to end up in the den glued to your big-screen TV, throwing back beers and watching every football game you can find.

What's going on here? Believe it or not, it's not as random or confusing as it might seem. Pleasure is the idol that's driving each of these specific behaviors, and as you can see, it can manifest itself in any number of ways. So an assault on pornography or gambling or video games isn't going to win the day. You had better aim the big guns at the idol of pleasure itself, or else the laundry list of sins that look very different from each other will just keep piling up.

So habit number one is to establish and maintain a wartime mentality. Let me get you started with three ways that you can do it.

Keep Soaking in God's Word

Hebrews 4:12–13 teaches:

> For the word of God is living and powerful, and sharper than any two-edged sword, piercing even to the division of soul and spirit, and of joints and marrow, and is a discerner of the thoughts and intents of the heart. And there is no creature hidden from His sight, but all things are naked and open to the eyes of Him to whom we must give account.

God's Word will show you what's in your heart. Reading the Bible keeps you honest, because you don't just read the Bible—the Bible reads *you*. It exposes you and leads you to freedom. Regular, daily Scripture intake can keep you from getting bogged down in the sins that so easily entangle you.

Look at some of the freedom that comes from God's Word:

> My soul is weary with sorrow;
> strengthen me according to your word.
> Keep me from deceitful ways;
> be gracious to me through your law.
> I have chosen the way of truth;
> I have set my heart on your laws.
> I hold fast to your statutes, O LORD;
> do not let me be put to shame.
> I run in the path of your commands,
> for you have set my heart free. (Ps. 119:28–32 NIV)

When you're feeding your idols—when you're preserving and protecting and promoting them—lying and deception are often part of the scenario, so God's Word frees you from idols of the heart by exposing the deception. The Holy Spirit uses Scripture as a spotlight to search the recesses of your heart where idols like to hide.

Psalm 119:42–45 says:

> Then I will answer the one who taunts me,
> for I trust in your word.
> Do not snatch the word of truth from my mouth,
> for I have put my hope in your laws.
> I will always obey your law,
> for ever and ever.
> I will walk about in freedom,
> for I have sought out your precepts. (NIV)

Keep soaking in God's Word; don't just read it. Chew on it; meditate on it. Pray it slowly back to God. Take a verse and hold it up in your mind, turning it slowly like some five-carat diamond, letting the light of the Holy Spirit do his job of refracting its truth like brilliant shafts of colored light down into your heart and soul, driving out the murky darkness where idols lurk. If you make this way of reading God's Word a habit, you won't have to go on an idol hunt every day. The light of God's Word will continually flush your idols out before they have time to entrench themselves in your life.

Keep Hanging with God's Family—the Church!

Another way to maintain a wartime mentality is to plug yourself in to a local church. Notice that I didn't say "attend"; I said "plug in to." There is a difference, and it will make all the difference in your fight against idols of the heart. You need the church—at close range—speaking into your life, even when it makes you uncomfortable. So when I tell you to plug in to a church, I don't mean to slip in and out of a Sunday-morning service, with a few handshakes and shallow "hellos." I'm talking about doing life together with a group of believers—being honest, sharing struggles, and, most importantly, giving a group of Christians permission to speak into your life when they see you beginning to veer off into something that would make you susceptible to sin. That's the church at its best, functioning as God designed it.

You can't do the work of detecting and destroying idols alone, sitting at home watching sermons on television. If you keep to yourself—out of church—you'll continually struggle to deal with the idols of your heart, with personal growth, and with repentance, because God didn't design you to live the Christian life alone. You need other Christians. But that concept runs counter to the current wave of Christian thinking here in America. Elyse Fitzpatrick describes it well:

> A number of years ago, my husband and I had the wonderful opportunity to vacation in Europe. In about three and a half weeks we visited thirteen different nations. When we'd enter a country, we'd get our passports stamped, exchange currencies, learn a few key phrases, and then off we'd go to visit the natives. We'd wander through outdoor markets, peruse museums, sample the cuisine. We'd exchange a few niceties with the locals, sit on the steps of cathedrals, watch the life of the town go by, take a picture or two, and purchase a little something to remind us of our time there, and then we were off. We had a wonderful vacation. Our hearts weren't changed in any significant ways by our little visits, but then they weren't meant to be. We were tourists. It seems to me that what I've just described is very close to many people's understanding of the

> congregational life of the local church. On any given Sunday, or better yet, Saturday night, many tourists can be found in church. They pop in for forty-five minutes or an hour, sing a chorus or two, exchange niceties with the locals: "Hi! How are you?" "Fine! How are you?" "Fine! Nice fellowshipping with you!" They sample some of the local cuisine, they might purchase a book or CD to remind them of their visit, and then they race to their cars to get to their favorite restaurant before the rush or home before the game. For many people, church is simply a place to go once a week. It is about being a tourist, and our land is filled with tourist-friendly churches. Pop in, pop out, do your religious thing, catch ya later![1]

Your idols blind you, but when you let people get close to you, they can see your idols better than you can. According to Proverbs 18:1, "A man who isolates himself seeks his own desire; he rages against all wise judgment." When you're serving your idols—doing what you want to do—you tend to pull away from other people. You don't want to be in a small group—you don't want to be accountable. Hebrews 10:25 says to "not forsake the assembling of ourselves together, as is the habit of some, but come together and look for ways to stir one another up to love and good deeds" (paraphrase). We need each other.

In most cases, others can see our lives better than we can, so humble yourself and invite the people closest to you to speak into your life, and ask them these questions:

- What do you see me running to instead of God?
- Where do you see a demanding spirit in me?
- What do you see me clinging to and craving more than God?
- Where do you see me wanting something so badly that I'm willing to sin to get it, or willing to sin if I think I'm going to lose it?

Keep Crying Out to God

A third way in which you can maintain a wartime mentality is to keep crying out to God. On the battlefield, soldiers understand how critical communication is. And that's one of the first things the enemy tries to cut off. Soldiers on the front line are more easily disheartened and confused if the enemy can disrupt communications between them and their commanders. It's no different with spiritual warfare. Our enemy is a master of war tactics. He strives to cut off communication between us and our heavenly Commander. Don't let it happen. Keep crying out to God. Keep praying Psalm 139:23–24: "Search me, O God, and know my heart; try me, and know my anxieties; and see if there is any wicked way in me, and lead me in the way everlasting."

HABIT #2: MAKE CHOICES THAT STARVE YOUR IDOLS

Every choice you make, even a little one, either feeds or starves your idols. So get used to the idea that there are no little choices. You have to think about the little stuff, because little stuff always turns into big stuff, because even little stuff comes from below the surface, from the heart. In Matthew 15:19–20, God tells us that "out of the heart proceed evil thoughts, murders, adulteries, fornications, thefts, false witness, blasphemies. These are the things which defile a man." That's why we've been doing all this excavation work—digging below the surface.

Live a Commandment-Oriented Life instead of a Feeling-Oriented Life

There are two approaches to life in our culture. The first is a commandment-oriented life, living the way that God tells us to live. The second is a feeling-oriented life, living by your feelings. And sadly, Christians can fall into the feeling-oriented trap as easily as anyone else. But God tells us to live a commandment-oriented life. Whatever God's Word says is what we should want to do, whether we feel like it or not.

First Samuel 13:12–13 gives us an example of feeling-oriented rather than commandment-oriented actions. King Saul was supposed to wait for Samuel the prophet to come and offer a sacrifice, but as he waited, Saul got scared when the Philistines began gathering for battle. And verse 12 informs us that Saul "felt compelled" and offered the sacrifice himself. But when Samuel arrived, he told the king, "You have done foolishly" (v. 13). So many times, when you do what you feel compelled to do, you act foolishly. If that feeling doesn't line up with God's Word, forget it—don't obey it; don't act on it. Often, to obey God's Word, you must do something that you don't feel like doing, or refrain from doing something that you feel like doing. Get used to it.

Learn to keep your feelings in their place. I'm not against feelings, nor is God. Just don't live by them—and don't let them rule you. To win the war against idols of the heart, you can't let feelings be the force that drives your choices. Obedience for the glory of God has to be what drives them. The good news is that *feelings follow obedience*, so you can obey your way into new feelings.

Eugene Peterson says:

> Feelings are great liars. . . . Feelings are important in many areas, but completely unreliable in matters of faith. . . . The Bible wastes very little time on the way we feel. . . . We think that if we don't feel something there can be no authenticity in doing it. But the wisdom of God says something different, namely, that we can act ourselves into a new way

of feeling much quicker than we can feel ourselves into a new way of acting.[2]

Pleasing God or Pleasing Self

So these are the two primary ways that people live. And that puts you at the *Y*, the fork in the road (see *Y* diagram). Every day you face dozens of choices, and each time you have to ask yourself, "Am I going to go with what I feel right now, or am I going to obey God? Am I going to please God or please myself?"

In the Old Testament, Joshua serves as a wonderful example when he tells the Israelites, "Choose for yourselves this day whom you will serve . . . But as for me and my house, we will serve the LORD" (Josh. 24:15). In other words, "we're going to serve God, not because we feel like it, not because our emotions are overwhelmingly in favor of it, but because God calls us to it."

All day long, you're faced with decisions: "What am I going to do? What am I going to think? How am I going to respond?" Romans 13:14 says, "But put on the Lord Jesus Christ, and make no provision for the flesh, to fulfill its lusts." So many times we make provision for the flesh, even if only in little ways. Don't do it! Make no provision for the flesh, to fulfill its lusts, because every decision, big or small, either feeds or starves your idols.

If you choose to please God, it will be hard, especially if you're already in the habit of living by your feelings, because by nature your sinful flesh recoils from the things of God. You're in Romans 7, where Paul says in verses 15 and 24, "The good that I want to do, I don't do. The very thing that I say I'm never going to do again, I keep doing. . . . Oh, who will deliver me from this body of death?" (paraphrase).

Biblical Counseling *Y* Diagram[3]

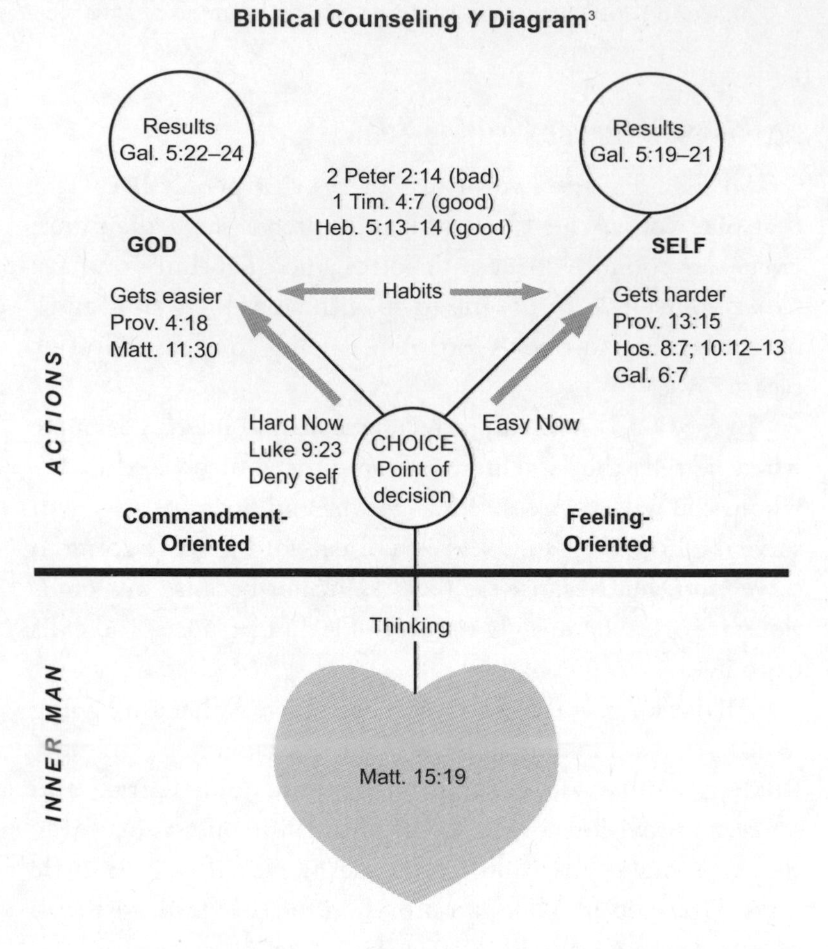

2 Cor. 5:9
Only two choices on the shelf: pleasing God or pleasing self

Keep Your Feelings Tethered to the Truth of God's Word

So many Christians shuffle through their lives in an unconscious stupor—susceptible to emotional highs and lows, beset with bouts of depression, anxiety, and worry—because their emotions are running loose, off the leash of the gospel. Your emotions need to be tied to God's truth, or else, like an unruly dog, they get loose and run wild around the neighborhood. Only God's Word can keep your emotions tethered and stable.

To change metaphors, God's Word and his gospel should be like an IV bag that keeps your soul hydrated with living water, steadily dripping the hope-giving, life-altering, joy-igniting, perspective-changing truth—truth that will *then* shape how you feel, regardless of what's going on around you, because it's based on the objective, unchanging truth of God's Word, instead of your ever-changing, easily deflated, and often misguided feelings.

Jesus said in John 8:31–32, 36:

> If you abide in My word, you are My disciples indeed. And you shall know the truth, and the truth shall make you free. . . . Therefore if the Son makes you free, you shall be free indeed.

It doesn't say that you'll *feel* anything. Feelings come and go, but Jesus said, "You shall know the truth, and the truth shall make you free." What you *know* determines how you live, and it will shape how you feel. Knowing God's truth brings freedom—including freedom from the prison of your own feelings.

I'm pressing this issue hard because of how devalued the concepts of objective thinking and propositional truth have become in our culture. People today—including Christians—think that whatever they *feel* is what's real. No—whatever God *says* is what's real. Pleasing self is easy because it's tied to your feelings. You think, "How could it be wrong if it feels so right?" Pleasing self takes no effort at all—you can just go with the flow—but that's not how it is with pleasing God.

Exercise Yourself to Godliness

As you cultivate the habit of pleasing God, it gets easier—not *easy*, but not as hard as it feels at first. For example, if you start exercising a new muscle—maybe doing curls with a dumbbell for your biceps—you'll think you're going to die when you wash your hair that first week. You never knew you could feel so much pain in one area of your body! But that bicep had been an unused muscle, one that you hadn't developed or used much. Yet if you keep exercising that muscle week after week, will it keep screaming in pain? Will you always think you're going to die when you wash your hair? No—it will get easier. Proverbs 4:18 says, "The path of the righteous grows brighter and brighter like the new dawn" (paraphrase). As you choose to please God, he promises you a path that will get brighter and brighter in his glory and presence.

Don't get me wrong; it will never be pain-free. There will be trials and troubles, but God gives us an open invitation to bring it all to him, "casting all your care upon Him, for He cares for you" (1 Peter 5:7). In Matthew 11:28, Jesus invites us to "come to Me, all you who labor and are heavy laden." And what is it that we're most burdened with? Our sin. But Jesus says:

> Come to Me, all you who labor and are heavy laden, and I will give you rest. Take My yoke upon you and learn from Me, for I am gentle and lowly in heart, and you will find rest for your souls. For My yoke is easy and my burden is light. (Matt. 11:28–30)

In Jesus' day, people would yoke an older ox to a younger one so that the young one could learn the ways of plowing. In these verses Jesus is saying, "Be yoked up with me and go through your day with me, and learn from me, for I am gentle and lowly in heart." And then he says, "My yoke is easy." In the Greek, the word translated "easy" means "a good fit." You might think your sin is a good fit, but its idolatrous yoke will chafe you more and more; the longer you wear it, the tighter it gets, and it will choke off your spiritual life. The sinful sores and choking fits caused by your idolatrous yoke will keep you walking with your head down, unable to breathe the fresh air of grace.

"Come to me," he says.

Whose yoke are you wearing right now? Is it a good fit? Has sin deceived you? Is the thing that you thought would lead to joy and freedom turning into a prison of your own making? That can all end today. Jesus is calling. He's ready to shatter the yoke of idolatrous sin in your life, and to take the yoke with you in a way that fits like nothing else. Don't you want that?

You Reap What You Sow

Life is still going to be hard. You'll still go through trials, but the one you're yoked with makes all the difference in how you go through it. Jesus' yoke is a good fit, and the path that he leads you on gets brighter and brighter.

On the other hand, pleasing self gets harder and harder. It starts off easy, and initially you make countless easy decisions, but those decisions will lead you through some of the hardest places you could imagine, through the heartbreak of broken relationships, and perhaps into consequences that can't be reversed. That's the deception and lie of sin. The first leg of the journey feels so easy, so effortless—just doing what you feel and what you want—but each step down that path slowly tightens the vise of sin, until it chokes grace and peace and freedom right out of your life.

Galatians 6:7 warns, "Do not be deceived, God is not mocked; for whatever a man sows, that he will also reap." There is going to be a harvest—and if you've been living to please yourself, the eventual harvest will be hard, painful, and messy. You'll wake up one day and say, "Why am I having all this trouble? This isn't what I want."

You're reaping what you've sown.

We want to sow to the flesh, but reap the fruit of the Spirit: love, joy, peace, patience, kindness, gentleness, and so on. But that's not how the spiritual harvest works—you reap what you sow. So the feeling-oriented life just gets harder and harder, even though it started off so easy. Proverbs 13:15 plainly states that "the way of the transgressor is hard" (ASV). Hosea 8:7 goes on to say, "They sow the wind, and reap the whirlwind." The rule of the harvest is that you will reap later than you sow, you'll reap more than you sow, and it will always cost you more than you wanted to pay. Always.

The way of transgressors is hard. And it's our idolatry that blinds us to so much of the sin that we're stumbling into.

God's Gift of Habit

God gave us a wonderful capacity to form habits. Habits don't have to be bad. You say, "Trying to please God is hard. Will it stay this hard forever?" No, it won't. With God's grace being poured out on you, his Holy Spirit living in you, and God's people surrounding you, you can form habits that please God. The ability to form habits is a wonderful gift from God. Without it, you would be wondering, "How do I put on my jeans? Do I put my left leg in first, or my right?" and "How do I dry off with a towel?" and "How does this toothbrush thing work?" But because God created habits, most of what you do, every day of your life, you don't even have to think about.

You can form righteous, godly habits. But don't hear me saying that you'll ever reach the point that your godly habits all become automatic. That's never going to happen in this life. If I stop thinking about how to love my wife, stop praying about it, stop purposing to do it, she'll become one very unloved woman. But I don't have to work at it as hard as I did twenty years ago, when we first started working on our marriage. At first I thought, "I can't do this, even if it *is* what God's Word says. It's just not me." Guess what? *Me* has changed. And so can you.

You don't have to keep being who you are. That's what the Holy Spirit is all about. That's what God's Word is all about—and prayer, and hanging with God's people. God is all about changing us—for his glory—into the image of his Son, Jesus Christ. So he gave us the capacity to form habits. Make habits work for you in this fight against sin and idols of the heart. Purpose that you're going to live a commandment-oriented life rather than a feeling-oriented life.

First Timothy 4:7 tells us to "exercise yourself toward godliness." Hebrews 5:14 also tells us about people "who by constant use have trained themselves to distinguish good from evil" (NIV). They did it by constant use, by exercising—by habit. Peter gives some bad examples; in 2 Peter 2:14 he speaks of people "having eyes full of adultery and that cannot cease from sin . . . They have a heart trained in covetous practices." Who trained their heart in covetous practices? They did. They behaved a certain way—the way their feelings were already moving—until it became a habit. They trained their hearts to sin.

So what are the results of pleasing God and living a commandment-oriented life? The fruit of the Spirit: love, joy, peace, patience, and more (see Gal. 5:22–23). And what are the results of pleasing self? Galatians 5 gives a list for that as well: adultery, fornication, sorcery, hatred, jealousies, selfish ambitions, angry outbursts, dissension, and so on, ad infinitum, ad nauseam.

Ken Collier explains, "There are only two choices on the shelf: pleasing God or pleasing self."[4] But we try to find some middle road, wanting to do a little of each. Yet there are only two choices. We should strive to emulate the apostle Paul when he says in 2 Corinthians 5:9, "Therefore we make it our aim, whether present or absent, to be well pleasing to Him."

Stop and think about your own life. Which way have you been turning each day as you face the fork in the road? Are you taking the easy path, giving in to your feelings? Or are you choosing to obey God's Word—even when it doesn't *feel* right to you?

HABIT #3: LEARN TO WORK BACKWARD FROM THE CHAOS IN YOUR LIFE TO YOUR OWN IDOLATROUS DESIRES

To detect and destroy idols in your life, you need to learn to ask yourself good questions, especially questions relating to heart motivation. Ken Sande in his book *The Peacemaker* gives some excellent diagnostic questions that you can use to work backward from the conflict to your idols:[5]

- What am I willing to sin to get?
- Why am I punishing this person?
- Why am I demanding?
- Why am I expecting so much from this person?
- Why do I have this conflict?

As Psalm 24:3–4 points out, "Who may ascend into the hill of the LORD? Or who may stand in His holy place? He who has clean hands and a pure heart, who has not lifted up his soul to an idol . . ."

Take some time to pray, "God, where is my heart divided? Where am I lifting up my soul to an idol, even a good one, such as wanting a godly husband, having obedient kids, or getting out of debt?"

Pray, "God, what about me? Lord, show me. The conflict between me and my siblings—or me and my spouse, or me and my boss—is it because of my idols?" What is God asking you to lay down? Give it up, and trust him to work in that area. He will!

AN EXAMPLE OF HOW IDOLATRY CAN DESTROY A HOME

Below is the testimony of a young wife in our church, who recognized that the idols of her heart were causing her to push away the very people she loved most—her husband and children. Beginning to detect and destroy the specific idols of her heart was a key part of what God used to change how she was relating to her family.

> Learning about idols of the heart exposed in me three big idols:
>
> 1. The obedience of my children—son and daughter, ages three and two
> 2. Trying to control my husband
> 3. My desire to never be disappointed
>
> So what were some of the indications that made me think that these were possible idols in my life?
>
> It occurred to me one day that I wasn't even enjoying my kids. I was reading books and taking parenting classes, trying to learn all I could to train them to be godly kids—but I wasn't enjoying

them. The real tip-off was when my three-year-old son started asking me, "Mommy, you're not mad at me?" He would even ask this randomly throughout the day when I wasn't disciplining him. I took this as a bad sign. With my kids, I had the expectation that they should obey me—and that they should obey me, right then and right there! And if they didn't, they'd get my wrath of impatience and anger. Little things like my son's knocking his sippy cup off the table just burned me up. At every meal, it seemed that he would inevitably knock his sippy cup from the table. And oh, my goodness, it was just like nails on a chalkboard. It was something so minor, but I was responding so impatiently because I wanted him to have self-control and just keep his sippy cup on the table. How hard could that be? I was an impatient person. He would not get into his car seat fast enough for me, and even though he was an energetic three-year-old boy, I expected him to stand perfectly still when I dressed him.

My husband and I were also arguing frequently about money—mainly my complaining about how he wasn't making enough so that I could stay home with the kids and not have to work, and my asking him, "When am I ever going to be able to homeschool them?" On top of that, we both had school debts that I was feverishly wanting to pay off. My husband was not making enough money to allow me to quit my job and stay home with my kids, and he wasn't making enough money to pay off my debts. So every time we broached the subject of work, or money, or debt, I would become angry and impatient, and it would turn into a big mess.

In the midst of all this conflict, God used a Sunday school class to remind me of Psalm 139:23–24:

Search me, O God, and know my heart;
    test me and know my anxious thoughts.
See if there is any offensive way in me,
    and lead me in the way everlasting. (NIV)

I started praying these verses every morning during my prayer time, and also whenever I'd just gotten angry with the kids or with my husband—and the Lord caused me to feel an overwhelming desire to change. The more I prayed, the more God began to show me that I was habitually impatient, angry, controlling, bitter, and mean-spirited with my kids and my husband. As my husband and I began marriage counseling in our church, I was further convicted by John 3:30: "He must become greater; I must become less" (NIV). I was convicted that night that not only were there patterns of sinful behavior stemming from pride and selfishness in my life, but also I was filled with unrealistic expectations toward people around me because I was clinging to the idol of "I must have a life free of disappointment."

An example of how these expectations led to continual disappointments in my marriage is that I wanted Craig to be ready to "step up to the plate," as I called it, and be a leader in our home and a leader in our church. That means that I wanted him to lead a small-group Bible study in our home and I wanted us to start counseling other couples together in our church.

But my husband told me that he was not, and still is not, ready to do this. When I would demand these things and they weren't met, I would either be angry and manipulative or be impatient and harsh, withholding my affection and love. This was the pattern of how I was relating to my husband and children.

My husband and I began counseling with a couple in our church, and our pastor was teaching on idols of the heart. I began to realize that the idols of my heart were driving me to sin to get what I wanted, or to sin if I didn't get what I wanted. So I asked myself, "If you're not going to enjoy your children now, and these issues are going to be so much bigger when they get older, when are you going to enjoy them? And when will my husband and I stop living like roommates and start enjoying each other's company, and have a close, intimate relationship again?" Most convicting of all, I realized, "I'm a Christian woman, and I'm supposed to be joyful. But why am I not joyful when I know I should and could be?" These questions started to prick me.

At this point, I decided that I was going to do whatever was necessary to change. I didn't want to live like this anymore, and I didn't want to be characterized by being harsh, critical, controlling, and mean-spirited—especially with my kids and my husband. I repented of my sinful behavior with the help of the godly couple who was counseling us. One night in our counseling session, I literally got down on my knees and I gave my kids, my husband, my finances, and my life to God. I said, "Take it all. Do whatever you need to do to change me, because I'm tired of being like this, and I know I'm not obeying you." I also asked God to help me to take the focus off my kids and my husband as the primary source of my fulfillment and joy, and to help me to find satisfaction in God alone. I realized for the first time that I had never done that.

In the days that followed, I attempted to put off anger and impatience and all the other sinful behaviors, and to put on the godly characteristics. Through counseling I had memorized Ephesians 4:22–24:

> You were taught, with regard to your former way of life, to put off your old self, which is being corrupted by its deceitful desires; to be made new in the attitude of your minds; and to put on the new self, created to be like God in true righteousness and holiness. (NIV)

Instead of attempting to obey verses 22 and 24 by just "putting off" and then "putting on," I started trying to obey verse 23, which talks about forming a new attitude in my mind. So I started asking myself two questions when I was tempted to get angry or impatient. As soon as I felt the anger or impatience starting to build, I would ask myself, "What am I wanting and what am I thinking right now?"

I asked myself these two questions multiple times throughout the day, whenever I started to feel angry and impatient. Not *after* a blowout, but *before*. And each time I stopped to ask myself these questions before reacting in anger, I saw a pattern. I was selfish and full of pride. I just wanted my way. I was perpetually choosing my needs and my plans and my time over my family's. In counseling I had also memorized Philippians 2:3–5:

> Do nothing out of selfish ambition or vain conceit, but in humility consider others better than yourselves. Each of you should look not only to your own interests, but also to the interests of others.
>
> Your attitude should be the same as that of Christ Jesus. (NIV)

I worked hard to change my thinking, by filtering all my decisions through these verses. I started thinking of Craig's and the kids' needs and desires more than my own. And practically speaking, when I felt myself getting angry or impatient, I would just look at what I was wanting and to see whether it pleased God. If it was focused on self more than pleasing God, I would choose to change my thinking and take another course of action, or I would change my tone of voice and the way I was about to react to my family. As I was starting to see how self-centered I was, I knew I needed God's strength for lasting change. I prayed for strength to obey God's Word and please God whether I felt like it or not.

Although my desire for my husband to lead a small group, to make more money, and to lead us into couples counseling hasn't changed, my attitude and actions are changing to please God rather than to please myself.

By God's grace, I'm forming a new habit of responding differently to my husband and children. Not long after God began doing this work in my heart, I had an opportunity to put into practice new behavior and to respond differently to my husband. My husband brought up the subject of karate and cable television. Both had been a source of real contention in our home. In an effort to cut costs, we'd canceled our cable television, and also because I'd told my husband that it was too great a temptation for me to just waste time when I have so many other things I need to be doing. Occasionally he would ask me about getting cable again and I would always say, "No, please don't get it." Well, on this particular day, he told me that he had ordered it and that it was coming on Saturday. I said, "Sweetheart, if at all possible, can I change your mind?" I said, "It's not about the money. It's only $13 a month. But it's such a temptation for me." At the same time, he also informed me that he was going back to karate, which would be a night away from me and the kids. Again I said, "Sweetheart, things right now between us are not great, and I would love to use that time to spend some more time with you. Would you please reconsider?" I made my appeal and he said, "No." He said, "I made a decision. I'm going back and we're getting cable."

But here's where it gets interesting. We were in bed that night, and what I did shocked even myself; I decided not to play possum. You know how you do that, ladies? You roll over. Well, I rolled—but I rolled *toward* my husband, and I put my arm on him and said, "Honey, I love you, and regardless of what you choose to do, I'm going to love you, and I'm not going to be bitter about this."

What a victory to respond in a new way that pleased God and didn't drive my husband further from me. I don't take credit for it. It was God's work in me. But I *did* have to make the choice to love my husband and to please God when I didn't get my way. Understand that the changes I've been experiencing are not possible without God's prompting or the power of his Holy Spirit working in me. I'm reminded of Ephesians 2:10: "For we are God's workmanship, created in Christ Jesus to do good works, which God prepared in advance for us to do" (NIV).

I'm not yet finished changing and growing, for I hope to never be satisfied with who I am in Christ until either he takes me home or he returns. Jeremiah 29:11–13 states:

> "For I know the plans I have for you," declares the LORD, "plans to prosper you and not to harm you, plans to give you hope and a future. Then you will call upon me and come and pray to me, and I will listen to you. You will seek me and find me when you seek me with all your heart." (NIV)

We can seek God with all our heart only after we choose to repent of our idols and start choosing to please God more than self. Doing so might just keep you from leading your own family down a path of destruction.

Part 3

SO WHAT DIFFERENCE WILL IT MAKE IN MY LIFE?

Chapter 13

What Would an Idol-Free Life Look Like?

As we wrap up this study, I hope you are getting excited about what will happen as a result of identifying and repenting of the idols of your heart, and what changes you can expect in your life.

You'll Start to Really Get Free

First, you'll start to become really free, maybe for the first time in your life. Yes, there's freedom in Christ as soon as you trust him for salvation, but if you're like most people, you came to Christ with baggage in the form of idolatry—baggage that didn't disappear the moment you put your trust in him. You're forgiven, the handwriting that was against you is canceled (Col. 2:14), but you don't feel totally free because you're still dragging your idols around with you.

But here's the good news: repenting of idols is where freedom really begins, freedom to serve God and freedom to run unhindered toward godliness. Hebrews 12:1–2 exhorts, "Since we are surrounded by so great a cloud of witnesses, let us lay aside *every weight*, and the sin which so easily ensnares us, and let us run with endurance the race that is set before us, looking unto Jesus, the author and finisher of our faith." What is the "every weight" that you need to lay aside? Idols—they're weighing you down. Yes, God saved you. Yes, his Spirit is in you. Yes, you want to please him. Yes, you want to pursue holiness. But you're trying to run the race while lugging along the weight of your idols.

Two problems are addressed in those verses: (1) idols weigh you down, and (2) idols keep you from seeing Jesus. You can't run, and you can't fix your eyes on Jesus, because your idols weigh you down and block your view. Ezekiel 14:3 says, "These men have set up their idols in their hearts, and put before them that which causes them to stumble into iniquity." Idols trip you up, because living with idols is like trying to run with your hand in front of your face. You might do it, but you'll stumble a lot, and you'll stumble into sin.

For example, let's consider a young couple who are caught up in sexual immorality—having sex or otherwise conducting themselves in an impure way before marriage. In many cases, even if they're both Christians, they won't stop even after hearing verses that say not to commit fornication and to keep themselves holy. Why not? Because the root issue is usually an idol of the heart, such as "I must have the affection of others" or "I must be noticed." Until these idols are addressed, the couple will keep stumbling into sexual immorality, because sexual pleasure is not *all* they want. Attention and affirmation are what they want. So until they repent of these root sins that lie unnoticed and unaddressed in their lives, and treasure Christ more fully, they'll just keep plunging further and further down the path of sexual sin.

YOU'LL HAVE A REVIVAL OF GRATITUDE FOR THE GOSPEL

The second thing you can look forward to as you repent of idolatry is that God shows you the ugliness of what's been going on inside you, and you find that it's far worse than those outward, obvious things that you've focused on before. And the more he shows you, the more level the ground at the foot of the cross starts to appear. You realize that you stand at the cross on level ground with prostitutes and gamblers, even rapists and murderers—even though, in your own mind, you had always kept yourself separated from such people in a category of your own, a category called "Not So Bad."

But coming to grips with the idols of *your own* heart shatters your pious categories and heightens your gratitude. Your opinion of yourself plummets, while your appreciation for the gospel soars. Coming face-to-face with your idols puts you in the same category of "Sinner" with everyone else, so that—maybe for the first time—you're able to thank God for the gospel and say, "*I* need the gospel. Christ died for *me*, not just people I thought were worse than me."

First Corinthians 1:17 says, "For Christ did not send me to baptize, but to preach the gospel—not with words of human wisdom, lest the cross of Christ be emptied of its power" (NIV). Our idols often empty the cross of Christ of its power by hindering us from seeing it. We don't rightly appreciate the power of the cross because we haven't rightly seen the ugliness of our hearts. Detecting and destroying idols can change that, but be careful—don't simply obsess over your own dark, ugly, sinful heart. Move on to the gospel, and rejoice!

And what is the gospel? The term *gospel* is shorthand for the work that Christ did for us—he died for sinners and then rose again on the third day in victory over Satan, hell, sin, and death. And he did it for people who don't deserve it—people such as you and me. Even if you've never murdered, raped, embezzled, or pillaged a village, you'll have a revival of gratitude for the gospel when you begin to see and repent of the idols in your life.

We're seeing a renewed emphasis these days on the need for believers to preach the gospel to themselves every day, but maybe you find it hard to get excited about it. Do this: for the rest of your life, look for idolatry in your heart every day, and you'll be running to the gospel every day—and you'll appreciate the gospel every day because you'll be freshly reminded every day why Christ had to die on the cross.

YOU MIGHT SEE CLEARLY FOR THE VERY FIRST TIME

Third, when you start detecting and destroying idols in your life, you'll see yourself and others around you more clearly. In Matthew 7:3–5, Jesus says:

> And why do you look at the speck in your brother's eye, but do not consider the plank in your own eye? Or how can you say to your brother, "Let me remove the speck from your eye"; and look, a plank is in your own eye? Hypocrite! First remove the plank from your own eye, and then you will see clearly to remove the speck from your brother's eye.

Many times, that plank in your eye is idolatry. Your idols form the plank you're walking around with—banging into people, banging into life, wondering why things are going so badly, and why you're surrounded by idiots. And all the while, you think you're the one with your head screwed on straight. But it's *your* idols, *your* craving, *your* demanding that are the problem. Now, with that backdrop, is it any wonder that you have conflict and problems with the people around you?

In the first couple of years of our marriage, while my heart was raging with my own idols and I didn't see it, I couldn't see clearly enough to talk to my wife about the ways I perceived her to be sinning against me. But that didn't stop me from trying! My idols twisted my perception of my wife and our marriage. My perception of our home was skewed because my idols had blinded me to my own sins and had exaggerated the sins of those around me. And with that kind of perception, it wasn't long before I felt angry, mistreated, and sorry for myself, thinking, "I deserve better than this. This is how she's going to treat me?" But don't smugly think how messed up I am. Whether you know it or not, your idols are doing the same thing to you in all your relationships.

YOU'LL FEEL MORE CONVICTION OF SIN

When you repent of idolatry, you'll feel more conviction for your sin, and you'll have the ability to forsake it. You'll be more sensitive to God's prompting and conviction. You might think, "Wait a minute . . . I don't think I want that." Oh, but you should! Beware of insensitivity to the Holy Spirit's conviction. Beware of spiritual callousness. Proverbs 28:13 teaches, "He who covers his sins will not prosper, but whoever confesses and forsakes them will have mercy." The mercy is not in confessing all day long, "Yeah, yeah, I did it again"; it's in *forsaking* your sin that you find mercy. Idolatry keeps you from taking the next step of forsaking sin. You're still clinging to the root idol that feeds that sin, still cherishing and protecting it, even while you confess the sin. You confess it; you acknowledge it as sin. But the idols of your heart tell you, "Don't let go. Hang on to it. You might need it again. Don't let go."

The Bible teaches that mercy is there for those who confess and forsake. François Fénelon wrote, "As the inner light increases, you will see the imperfections which you have heretofore seen as basically much greater and more harmful than you had seen them up to the present." When you start repenting of idols, you'll have a lower opinion of yourself. You'll see things that you didn't see before—things you thought were no big deal—with a heightened awareness of your sinfulness. He continues, "But this experience, far from discouraging, will help to uproot all your self-confidence, and to raze to the ground the whole edifice of pride. Nothing marks so much the solid advancement of a soul, as this view of his wretchedness without anxiety and without discouragement."[1]

Notice: "without anxiety and without discouragement." Every time you see your own wretchedness, you can say, "Yes! That's why I have a Savior. That's why I have a robe of righteousness that's not my own. That's why Christ went to the cross." When you see your wretchedness, it doesn't flatten you in despair if you understand grace and the cross that stands at the heart of the gospel. But when you're trying, in your pride and self-righteousness, to keep up appearances, and God shows you who you really are, it prostrates you in a self-condemning funk. You wallow in despair over sin that you can't get free from.

But when you understand the freedom that comes in being brought low by a loving God, you can revel in him and say, "Here I am at my lowest point, along with all those who have reviled God and turned away from him. I'm here and I'm happy, because here's my Savior, here's grace, here's the cross."

YOUR PASSION AND LOVE FOR GOD WILL SOAR!

Finally, let's look at Luke 7:36–38:

> Then one of the Pharisees asked Him [Jesus] to eat with him. And He went to the Pharisee's house, and sat down to eat. And behold, a woman in the city who was a sinner, when she knew that Jesus sat at the table in the Pharisee's house, brought an alabaster flask of fragrant oil, and stood at His feet behind Him weeping; and she began to wash His feet with her tears, and wiped them with the hair of her head; and she kissed His feet and anointed them with the fragrant oil.

In Jesus' day, people didn't sit around a table as we do, on chairs that scooted underneath it. Their table was much lower than ours, and they reclined on their sides around it. In verse 37 we see "a woman in the city who was a sinner." Now, we're all sinners, but this means that she was renowned for sin, perhaps a prostitute. So Jesus was at the head at the table, with this woman at his feet. She was weeping so profusely that her tears were falling from her face onto his dusty feet, and she wiped his feet with her hair.

The scene continues in verse 39:

> Now when the Pharisee who had invited Him saw this, he spoke to himself, saying, "This man, if He were a prophet, would know who and what manner of woman this is who is touching Him, for she is a sinner."

Jesus had been invited to this meal primarily out of curiosity, so that the Pharisee could decide what he thought about him. The man thought, "Jesus is no prophet if he's letting this sinful woman touch his feet."

Look what happened next:

> Jesus answered and said to him, "Simon, I have something to say to you." So he said, "Teacher, say it."
>
> "There was a certain creditor who had two debtors. One owed five hundred denarii, and the other fifty. And when they had nothing with which to repay, he freely forgave them both. Tell Me, therefore, which of them will love him more?"
>
> Simon answered and said, "I suppose the one whom he forgave more." And He said to him, "You have rightly judged." Then He turned to the woman, and said to Simon, "Do you see this woman?" (Luke 7:40–44)

Jesus was asking Simon, "Do you see that she's a person, that she's created in the image of God?" All Simon saw was a sinner. All he saw was her reputation. All he saw was a false standard that placed him far above her.

Jesus continued:

> Do you see this woman? I entered your house; you gave Me no water for My feet, but she has washed My feet with her tears and wiped them with the hair of her head. You gave Me no kiss, but this woman has not ceased to kiss My feet since the time I came in. You did not anoint My head with oil, but this woman has anointed My feet with fragrant oil. Therefore, I say to you, her sins, which are many, are forgiven, for she loved much. (Luke 7:44–47)

Notice those two words, *many* and *much*. Don't misunderstand the passage; the woman's many sins are not forgiven because she loved much. Her loving much is the evidence of her having been forgiven her many sins.

Finally, Jesus told Simon, "But to whom little is forgiven, the same loves little" (Luke 7:47).

Jesus was telling him, "Look at this woman's passion, her love, her worship. Then look at your own in comparison. When you think you don't have much to be forgiven of, you don't love very much."

May we forever be passionate about the Lord Jesus Christ, passionate in our worship, passionate in sharing with other people the story of Christ and forgiveness. May we forever be passionate and compassionate in coming alongside those who are overtaken in a trespass, because every day we are mindful and aware that we have been forgiven *much*. And may we love much.

When you repent of the idols of your heart, when you stay constantly aware of just how much you've been forgiven, you love much. You can't be more loving by trying to drum up more feelings. Rather, look at your sin, and consider all that God has forgiven you. And as you repent of idols of your heart and cultivate a lifestyle of repentance, you'll have a lifestyle of love.

So the message I'm giving you in this final chapter is a message of hope. Don't focus on others around you. Don't live in the past. Turn off *Dr. Phil*, put down that best seller, pick up the Bible, and find the hope, help, and grace that flow from the cross.

NOTES

Chapter One: Idolatry Starts with Gospel Drift

1. C. J. Mahaney, *The Cross Centered Life* (Colorado Springs: Multnomah Books, 2002), 20–21.

2. David Powlison, "Idols of the Heart and Vanity Fair," *Journal of Biblical Counseling* 13, no. 2 (Winter 1995): 35.

Chapter Two: Idolatry Is an Inside Job

1. Paul David Tripp, *Lost in the Middle* (Wapwallopen, PA: Shepherd Press, 2004), 275–76.

2. Richard Keyes, "The Idol Factory," in *No One but God: Breaking with the Idols of Our Age*, eds. Os Guinness and John Seel (Chicago: Moody Press, 1992), 31–32.

3. Ibid., 32.

4. Quoted in Donald W. McCullough, *The Trivialization of God: The Dangerous Illusion of a Manageable Deity* (Colorado Springs: NavPress, 1995), 106.

5. David Powlison, "The Sufficiency of Scripture to Diagnose and Cure Souls," *Journal of Biblical Counseling* 23, no. 2 (Spring 2005): 6.

6. Ibid.

7. Adapted from David Powlison, "X-Ray Questions: Drawing Out the Whys and Wherefores of Human Behavior," *Journal of Biblical Counseling* 18, no. 1 (Fall 1999): 4–7.

Chapter Three: Enough Is Never Enough

1. David Powlison, "Idols of the Heart and Vanity Fair," *Journal of Biblical Counseling* 13, no. 2 (Winter 1995): 1.

2. Ed Welch, "Motives: Why Do I Do the Things I Do?" *Journal of Biblical Counseling* 22, no. 1 (Fall 2003): 7.

Chapter Four: Idolatry Wreaks Havoc in Your Relationships

1. Paul David Tripp, *Instruments in the Redeemer's Hands* (Phillipsburg, NJ: P&R Publishing, 2002), 75, 106–7.

2. Dave Harvey, *When Sinners Say "I Do"* (Wapwallopen, PA: Shepherd Press, 2007), 69.

3. David Powlison, *Seeing with New Eyes* (Phillipsburg, NJ: P&R Publishing, 2003), 151.

4. Elyse Fitzpatrick and Jim Newheiser, *When Good Kids Make Bad Choices* (Eugene, OR: Harvest House, 2005), 56.

5. Concept taken from Paul Tripp, *Instruments in the Redeemer's Hands* (Phillipsburg, NJ: P&R Publishing, 2002), 85–88.

Chapter Five: Idolatry Changes Your Identity

1. Paul David Tripp, *Lost in the Middle* (Wapwallopen, PA: Shepherd Press, 2004), 276.

2. Paul David Tripp, *Instruments in the Redeemer's Hands* (Phillipsburg, NJ: P&R Publishing, 2002), 73.

3. Tripp, *Lost in the Middle*, 275.

4. Ibid., 275–76.

Chapter Six: We Need an X-Ray of the Heart

1. Paul David Tripp, *Lost in the Middle* (Wapwallopen, PA: Shepherd Press, 2004), 19.

Chapter Seven: Follow the Trail of Your Time, Money, and Affections

1. Richard Keyes, "The Idol Factory," in *No One but God: Breaking with the Idols of Our Age*, eds. Os Guinness and John Seel (Chicago: Moody Press, 1992), 31–32.

2. Louie Giglio, *The Air I Breathe: Worship as a Way of Life* (Colorado Springs: Multnomah Publishers, 2006), 10–11.

Chapter Eight: Look for Chaos!

1. Ed Welch, "Motives: Why Do I Do the Things I Do?" *Journal of Biblical Counseling* 22, no. 1 (Fall 2003): 7.

Chapter Nine: Don't Dare Follow Your Heart

1. Scotty Smith, *The Reign of Grace* (New York: Howard Books, 2003), 160–61.

2. Concept by Jay Adams, refined and developed by Lou Priolo.

Chapter Ten: Recognize Where Your Heart Is Most Vulnerable

1. *Calvin: Institutes of the Christian Religion*, ed. John T. McNeill, in *The Library of Christian Classics*, vol. XX, trans. Ford Lewis Battles (Philadelphia: The Westminster Press, 1960).

2. David Powlison, "The Sufficiency of Scripture to Diagnose and Cure Souls," *Journal of Biblical Counseling* 23, no. 2 (Spring 2005): 9–10.

3. David Powlison, "X-Ray Questions: Drawing Out the Whys and Wherefores of Human Behavior," *Journal of Biblical Counseling* 18, no. 1 (Fall 1999): 7.

Chapter Eleven: Let God Be God!

1. Leslie Vernick, *How to Find Selfless Joy in a Me-First World* (Colorado Springs: WaterBrook Press, 2003), 32–33.

2. Ibid., 126, quoting Oswald Chambers, *My Utmost for His Highest* (Urichsville, OH: Barbour and Co., 1963), 251.

3. C. J. Mahaney, *The Cross Centered Life* (Colorado Springs: Multnomah Books, 2002), 27–30.

4. Wayne Brown, *Water from Stone* (Colorado Springs: NavPress, 2004), 103.

5. Ibid., 104–5.

6. Arthur Bennett, ed., *Valley of Vision* (East Peoria, IL: Versa Press), 71.

Chapter Twelve: God's Prescription for Freedom

1. Elyse Fitzpatrick, *Because He Loves Me: How Christ Transforms Our Daily Life* (Wheaton, IL: Crossway Books, 2008), 173–74.

2. Eugene H. Peterson, *A Long Obedience in the Same Direction: Discipleship in an Instant Society* (Nottingham: IVP Books, 2000), 49–50.

3. Original concept by Ken Collier, director, The Wilds, Brevard, North Carolina; refined and developed by Mark Dutton, pastor, Faith Counseling Ministry, Lafayette, Indiana.

4. As quoted by Mark Dutton, in personal correspondence with the author.

5. Ken Sande, *The Peacemaker* (Grand Rapids: Baker Books, 2004), 173.

Chapter Thirteen: What Would an Idol-Free Life Look Like?

1. Quoted in C. J. Mahaney, *The Idol Factory* (Gaithersburg, MD: Sovereign Grace Ministries, 2001), audio sermon series, available at http://www.sovereigngraceministries.org.